'Traction Tin

An Early BR Traction Miscellany
Compiled by Andrew Royle

The · Transport · Treasury

Nos. D5501 and D5505 receive servicing on the fuelling roads at Stratford MPD. As both locomotives look remarkably clean, it is safe to assume that this photo was taken in 1958 and, incidentally, close to the photographer's birthplace. (Roy Vincent V255/1)

© Images and design: The Transport Treasury 2020. Text Andrew Royle.

ISBN 978-1-913251-09-3

First Published in 2020 by Transport Treasury Publishing Ltd. 16 Highworth Close, High Wycombe, HP13 7PJ

www.ttpublishing.co.uk

Printed in the UK by Henry Ling Limited, at the Dorset Press, Dorchester. DT1 1HD.

Contents

Front cover: The 4 May 1962 finds two new BRCW Type 2s on Cricklewood depot paired up (with connecting doors utilised) for duty on express passenger services between St Pancras and Nottingham. D5381 was to transfer to Scotland in 1970, whilst D5383 was written off after collision damage near Market Harborough in August 1965. Scottish preference was for sliding cab windows, but the Midland batch were given droplights. (Alec Swain L76-3)

Title page: EM1 class locomotive No. 26011 pulls away from Penistone with a train of steel in September 1954. When fully extended, the pantographs would almost be as tall as the locos themselves. The decision to electrify the route between Manchester, Sheffield and Wath was driven by its heavy freight traffic; much of this consisted of coal mined in the Yorkshire pits and steel that was produced in the Sheffield and Rotherham area for use in manufacturing west of the Pennines. Amongst other things in the right background, the posters advertise Mackeson (a stout beer popular until the 1970s) and Daz washing powder (which 'boils whitest of all'). A steam loco can be glimpsed on the line to Huddersfield and it is interesting that the telegraph poles and wires are still in use; wherever 25kV electrification was installed on the railway, there was no place for them. (Eric Blakey)

Rear cover: An unusual visitor to the yard at Crewe South depot on 12 February 1967 is Southern DC electric No. E5003 of the 'HA' type. Not apparent is the collision damage to the loco on the other side; this had led to it being sent north for a stay in Crewe Works, where it would become the seventh of its type to be put through re-conversion to an electro-diesel as E6107. A need for a batch of more powerful electro-diesels had been identified for the Bournemouth electrification scheme. The decision had been made that taking just ten of the poorer condition 'HA' types (eventually class 71) and converting them into 'HB' types (class 74) would be marginally cheaper than going for a completely new build. However, retaining the 'booster' system inherent in their design gave rise to space problems within the body plus the modification work also took longer than anticipated; the greater expense incurred therefore brought into question the wisdom of the original decision. Problematic in service because of their early electronic control system and comparing poorly with the more reliable 'JA' (class 73), these class 74s were withdrawn as soon as the Southern Region felt that they could do without them. The non-converted class 71s were to follow them into oblivion not long after, apart from the preserved E5001. (Eric Sawford ES6036)

Clearly not satisfied with BR's choice for its standard design of diesel-electric shunter, English Electric sought to try out a 500hp 0-6-0 design in 1956. It produced two similar locomotives, one with electric transmission and the other with hydraulic, the power unit itself being an uprated version of the six-cylinder one used in the class 08. This may have been an early attempt at determining which type of transmission was the better, at least in the lower power range. In the summer of 1959, No. D226 is seen carrying out station pilot duties at Liverpool Street station. The positioning of the fuel tank behind the cab would seem rather dubious, from a safety point of view. Perhaps qualifying as one of the earliest of preserved modern traction in the UK, D0226 (as it became in 1959 to avoid confusion with the newer type 4 D226. The locomotive seen here ended up moving to the Keighley & Worth Valley Railway in 1966, where it has worked ever since. The hydraulic version was scrapped. (Jim Harbart FH1577)

Introduction

The Transport Treasury archive tells a railway story which is dominated by steam traction. In the 1950s, most railway photographers were aware that change was coming and being enthusiasts, understandably tended to concentrate on recording what they thought was going to disappear. However, closer inspection of many collections in the archive reveals that not all chose to keep their lenses capped whenever a DMU or any other form of modern traction hove into view.

We are certainly lucky that men such as Dr Ian Allen and Alec Swain made a point of recording the railway scene, whatever the motive power involved, but others would also take the odd shot of modern traction too. Whether they did it to finish a particular roll of film, exercise their camera or even to stave off boredom, they often unwittingly captured railway scenes that would come and go in a remarkably short period of time.

Dieselisation of lines in the late 1950s/ early 1960s period often provided scant relief from the shadow of the Beeching Plan of course, so views of DMUs at Verney Junction or class 21s in Aberdeenshire are now just as fascinating as any that featured steam. Readers are invited to study the Transport Treasury website to gain a flavour of what is in the archive.

This book is a selection of views which have stood out to me as being of interest to both the railway historian and modeller. I have deliberately sought out some of the lesser known diesel shunters, together with locations on lines which either no longer exist or have changed out of all recognition on today's network. Also, expect to see certain classes of locomotive that were clearly off their beaten track. I have been keen to include shots which feature railway staff going about their work, as well as passengers or onlookers; this can remind us how fashions have changed over the years. For example, at the beginning of the 1960s, it was unusual to see a man in public without a hat but by the end of the decade, the situation was practically reversed!

The quality of the photographs inevitably varies much more than we are used to seeing today. It can be frustrating to find something quite unique in the archive, only to realise that the image itself is blurred or poorly exposed. We forget that photography was something that wasn't affordable to many and not everyone possessed a camera with a quality lens and shutter speed sufficient to arrest all movement, quite apart from the skills required to use a light meter. Even the famous names went through a learning process in their photography!

Whilst trying to write as objectively as possible, my own take on what is seen is bound to show through and I hope that readers will forgive that approach – you will doubtless have your own views too. It has been a fascinating and enjoyable task, both to put together the selection of photographs and to carry out the research necessary to provide relevant detail for their captions.

Andrew Royle

High Wycombe, January 2020.

Diesel Multiple Units

Above: Deemed as BR's first experiment to turn around the fortunes of a heavily loss-making branch line using modern traction, in the summer of 1956 two Derby 'Lightweight' single unit railcars were introduced between Banbury (Merton Street) and Buckingham. Appearing to be popular with passengers, Nos. M79900 & M79901 usually ran alone but would often need to couple up as a twin unit on market days and Saturdays. At first, M79901 was configured slightly differently to its twin, having greater luggage space and seating for 52 passengers, instead of 61. The other unit was later modified to match. However, despite a quoted one-third reduction in running costs and a considerable overall increase in patronage (up to a 400% improvement was quoted, set against the previous steam-operated service), the line still didn't pay its way; the service was discontinued in January 1961 following a twelve month reprieve when a bus replacement couldn't be arranged. After this the railcars continued to operate between Buckingham and Bletchley. M79900 is shown departing from underneath the roofless Banbury (Merton Street) station on a damp 26 November 1960. Note the low wooden platform with access steps - likely a nuisance at busy periods. (Dick Riley RCR15494)

Opposite top: Unit E79022 leads a two car 'Derby Lightweight' set forming this Cleethorpes-bound service at Grimsby Docks, where it also appears to be attracting the attention of railway staff on the opposite platform. The photo is undated but probably taken around 1955-56. With only the front vehicle powered by twin 150hp engines and an extra tail-load of a van at the rear, performance was unlikely to have been swift though still acceptable for the time. Early builds of these DMUs had three panes of glass in the front; this one has the modification of a horizontal member upon which the windscreen wiper module is fitted. The enormous poster on the right ('mark of a thousand good things') is advertising the Co-Operative Wholesale Society, later to be known simply as the 'Co-Op'. (Roy Vincent REV99-1)

Opposite bottom: An early 60s view of a two-car set pulling into Middle Drove station in the Fens with a Kings Lynn – March service. Note the yellow diamond multiple-unit coupling code on the front of the set and the single line token hoop on the driver's desk. Introduced before BR's 1955 Modernisation Plan, these units were early withdrawals from the fleet, once the requirement for rolling stock declined; they did not receive a classification under TOPS. Features of note are the tidy collection of fire buckets hanging on the side of the station cottage and the substantial reinforced concrete gateposts from which full width crossing gates are hung. The longevity of such gateposts (some still in use today) can be attributed to the work of railway engineer William Marriot, once of the Midland & Great Northern Railway. The Magdalen Road to Wisbech line closed in 1968. One platform of Middle Drove station still exists but with agricultural land much in demand in this flat and fertile landscape, elsewhere the route of the railway has disappeared under the plough in many places. (Dr Ian Allen D1644)

Opposite top: Still in East Anglia, one of the products of D Wickham & Co. (of Ware, Hertfordshire) arrives at Clare station in the Stour Valley, bound for Sudbury. Five of these two-car sets were ordered by BR and their exterior and interior design was quite different to that of most of the other first generation DMUs. They became class 109 and one went on to serve as the Eastern Region General Manager's Saloon in the 1970s, after the rest of the fleet had been withdrawn. It is now preserved on the Llangollen Railway. The blue square coupling code can be noted at either side of the yellow warning panel. All the usual features of a sleepy country station are on display here, from the tidiness of the signage to the kettle in the signal box. Although the line was closed through here, the expansion of nearby Haverhill in recent years has led to proposals to re-open the entire Stour Valley route, potentially linking Colchester with Cambridge once again. (Paul Hocquard)

Opposite bottom: On the evening of 17 June 1961, a half-day railtour organised by the Sheffield branch of the RCTS concludes its itinerary at Chesterfield Central. The 'North Derbyshire Railtour' had begun a short distance away at the Midland station at 1.30pm and traversed a variety of local lines, now long since closed. Central station itself would close to passenger traffic in March 1963, though the goods yard alongside it (to the left) would remain open for a few years after. The Trebor Sweets factory is prominent behind the train; some may recall the TV commercial from the 1960s, featuring a crowd singing that 'Trebor mints are a minty bit stronger'. The type of DMU seen here, consisting of cars 50036/56036, was one of the all-steel Derby 'Heavyweight' types (later class 114) which dominated local services in the Lincoln district for many years. (David Horne)

Above: Verney Junction was on a closed route which is now certain to re-open as part of the Oxford to Cambridge scheme. This place was one of those railway junctions in the middle of nowhere that would only come to life when a train passed through or called there; the rest of the time, the sounds of the countryside would only be interrupted by the occasional clank of a signal being pulled off. The train featured is working from Oxford to Cambridge and is one of the second design of 'Derby Lightweight' units (class 108 under TOPS) which were of a shorter length - 57ft 6in long instead of the 64ft of other similar designs. When the photo was taken in March 1960, this line was considered a very important cross-country link, particularly for freight and a marshalling yard was once planned just a few miles away from here at Swanbourne, near to the Bletchley flyover. Beyond the signal box, the line to Buckingham and Banbury can be glimpsed branching off to the right and a very elaborate form of metal chimney is evident on the roof of the eastbound platform waiting room. (Donald Robertson DR52-3)

Above: Savernake (pronounced 'savver-knack') in Wiltshire was once the site of a complex of junctions between the Great Western's Reading-Taunton (Berks & Hants) main line and the Swindon-Andover section of the Midland & South Western Junction Railway. On 21 June 1961, we see a train crossing from the down to the up main at Savernake Low Level, probably having worked a terminating service from Reading and now preparing to work back. The line going off to the right met the MSWJ avoiding line in the distance en route to Marlborough, from which direction another train is signalled, destined for the Low Level's bay platform. The 3-car DMU illustrated is one of the Pressed Steel Suburban units (built at the Linwood Works in Scotland) that served the lines out of Paddington for many years, becoming class 117. The train is precisely above the route of the Bruce Tunnel on the Kennet & Avon Canal, completed in 1809 and named after the local landowner who didn't want a deep cutting passing through his land. (David Horne)

Opposite top: The Gloucester Railway Carriage & Wagon Company built twenty of these single car DMUs for service in the Birmingham and Thames Valley areas. Here we see one of the Tyseley-allocated batch 'W55004' getting away from a bay platform at Birmingham Snow Hill on 21 March 1960, headed for Dudley. With a plume of exhaust adding to the smoggy central Birmingham sky, the driver has probably just engaged second gear with his right hand and is now re-applying power with the controller to his left. These units proved popular with crews, passengers and management alike as they were pleasant to travel in, as well as easy and economical to operate. Several are in use to this day on preserved railways, more than sixty years after they were introduced. The photo was taken from the steps of the station's North signal box. The case for the rundown of this magnificent station was easy to make in the 1960s but proved short-sighted; today's much smaller modern replacement now struggles to handle the passenger traffic on offer. The last service to run from the old station in 1972 was that to Wolverhampton Low Level (departing from the same bay platform we see being used here) by which time Snow Hill had become one enormous un-staffed halt! (Dick Riley RCR14547)

Opposite bottom: The first built 'bubble car' (as they were nicknamed) 'W55000' sits in platform 5 at Paddington, together with sister unit W55012, ready to work the 1.42pm to Reading on 14 October 1959. Each are coupled to single-ended trailer cars of a type that was designed especially for them; able to accommodate 95 passengers, against 65 for the double-ended cars, these were in the 56291 to 56299 series and produced in the same factory by Gloucester RCW Co. The fifteen single unit vehicles were moved around the system quite a lot, as they frequently came to be used as a last resort on branch lines under threat of closure. W55000 was a favourite on the Kingsbridge branch before services ended in September 1963 – it is now resident at the South Devon Railway, only a few miles away. The writer also fondly recalls seeing a then Tyseley-based M55012 leaving Leamington Spa for Stratford on Avon in the mid-1970s, often just minutes after a Western-hauled service for Birmingham New Street had departed. All were to become class 122 under TOPS. (Nick Nicolson LN2/32/3)

Opposite page: Taken on 11 September 1960 at Swindon Works, this close-up view shows the detail on part of one of the sister 'bubble car' variety, built by Pressed Steel of Linwood. Their headcode panels and 'cut off' buffer heads helped to tell them apart from the Gloucester product. Sixteen were produced in the number series 55020 to 55035, together with ten trailer cars, 56280 to 56289. Eventually class 121, their service life was similar to that of the Gloucester railcars, with re-use as route learners and sandite laying vehicles being a common form of redeployment, once they were no longer needed to carry passengers. The non-powered Driving Trailers (DTS) vehicles were similarly mostly withdrawn well before the double-ended cars. W55020 however led something of a charmed life and would return to passenger service in 2003, not finally finishing on the national network until 2017! (Alec Swain J46-4)

Above: It's fair to say that in the 1960s, derailments were a common occurrence on the railways. Breakdown cranes and recovery equipment trains were a fixture in the sidings of most large locomotive depots. There were also all manner of minor collisions and sideswipes which provided regular business for the railway workshops that existed across the country. What were the reasons for this? The list would be very long, if you compiled one but certainly there was far more acceptance back then that 'accidents will happen' – today, the prevailing view is that all accidents are preventable. Be that as it may, it is unlikely you would see a scene like this nowadays. For a start, there would probably be a wide and cordoned off safety zone extending beyond the boundary fence with sightseers kept well away. With no hard hats to be seen and only a few men wearing the small hi-vi vests that were just coming into use at that time, DMU vehicle Sc56481 is being recovered near to Dundee West shed on 20 July 1966. Built by Cravens of Sheffield, this was a non-powered DTC(L) – Driving Trailer Composite (with Lavatory). The Rolls-Royce engines in their twinned motor vehicles gave much trouble, hence these DMUs had all been withdrawn by 1970. (George Bett GCB674B)

In the time before Britain had any motorways, there was only one affordable means of transporting parcels around the country and that was by rail. Some of this traffic, particularly around the larger conurbations, was sufficiently important to warrant the use of dedicated vehicles such as this Great Western design of railcar. No. W34W was built at Swindon in 1941 but by the time this shot was taken at Paddington on 9 September 1959, it had just a few months of service remaining; in common with the other parcels-only railcar W17W which operated in the Thames Valley area, it was replaced by a new design of vehicle from Gloucester RC&W. Paddington's Goods Station dominates the background. (Eric Sawford ES4253)

W55993 was one of those new Gloucester-built parcels railcars mentioned opposite, although it entered service in the Birmingham area (two were shedded at Tyseley) and is shown departing from Snow Hill station on 21 March 1960. The website *Railcar.Co.Uk* informs us that no less than three different types of speed whisker were applied across the ten vehicles in the class! This example has the gangway cover variety with single stripes. Another was given double stripes for a time, while the four non-gangwayed ones supplied to the LMR had 'split' whiskers – one under each cab window. This picture is also a reminder of how station throats used to look. A complex layout with dozens of sets of switches, all aimed at maximum flexibility of working. When so many trains were loco-hauled and motive power swaps were frequent, then this kind of trackwork was important. However, it also demanded frequent and manpower intensive maintenance. (Dick Riley RCR 14553)

Opposite top: 'Too little, too light and too late' was the title of an article in the January 1968 issue of *'Railway Magazine'*. Written by John M Tolson, it was an interesting account that described the experiment of employing diesel railbuses on a range of rural branch lines across the country. Orders from five different manufacturers were placed in 1957. E79963 was one of the five vehicles purchased from the German company, Waggon und Maschinenbau (based on an already successful model) and put into service in East Anglia in July 1958; it is shown heading away from the camera at the branch terminus of Maldon East on 5 October 1963. Not obviously apparent is the fact that the buffer on the left is convex while the one to the right is flat; the other designs weren't given buffers at all so could not couple up or take a trailing load. By this stage, its original 150hp Buessing power unit had been replaced by a similar AEC engine that would have been easier and cheaper to maintain. Although the overall experiment might have been regarded as a failure, this particular brand of railbus has done quite well when you consider that four out of the original five are still in use to this day in preservation! E79963, for one, resides at the East Anglian Rail Museum at Chappel & Wakes Colne. (Alec Swain O59-1)

Opposite bottom: The railbus from Wickhams utilised a less powerful 105hp Meadows engine (the same as in its track recording car, covered above), though in a design that was very light in construction. In June 1959, Sc79967 waits in the grand setting of Crieff station before working to the junction at Gleneagles. The Crieff Junction railway encompassed stations that had wonderful names such as Tullibardine and Highlandman – sadly these were all to close in July 1964. Scotland too was where most railbus working was to be found, overall. So what was to be concluded from the railbus experiment? Apart from reliability issues and the fact that four of the five designs weren't flexible enough to couple up to anything else when traffic demanded, they weren't especially comfortable to ride in and struggled to accommodate heavy luggage, prams or bicycles. Whilst clearly cheap to operate in themselves, the savings they offered over other trains weren't enough to reprieve the majority of the unremunerative routes over which they ran (with the exception of the Braintree branch), often because insufficient economies were made to fixed costs. If some lines had been properly converted to light-rail operation at the same time, the story might have been different. (George Bett GCB655)

Above: The Elliott Track Recording Coach No. DB999507 was described in the September 1959 issue of *'Trains Illustrated'* magazine. Constructed by Wickhams of Ware, it weighed 24 tons and was powered by a Meadows 97hp diesel engine, enabling it to achieve a top speed of 55mph – normal track recording speed was 30mph. A separate generator was used to power its heating, lighting and equipment. A lattice girder framework was hung about its four axleboxes, upon which its track monitoring devices were mounted. Cooking, washing and toilet facilities were provided for the crew. An extra windscreen wiper will be noted on one of the side windows. Liveried in yellow, and brown with red bufferbeams, the compact unit is seen on display at Marylebone station on 14 July 1959. It was to see a variety of testing roles up until the early 1990s as 'Laboratory 20' and is now based at the Lavender Line (Sussex) in a passenger carrying role. (Nick Nicolson LN2030)

Above: This is one of those images for which we have some information but the accuracy of it is questionable. The description says that this is an 'Up driver training special'. However, the train (a reduced formation, led by a brand new W52086) is on the down road at Laira, so it could have been in the process of manoeuvring in readiness to return eastwards mid-run. The photographer, Alec Swain, was involved in the crew training and had quite likely detrained in order to take his shot on 29 May 1963. These WR-based sets were subsequently employed on Cardiff to Plymouth and Cardiff to Portsmouth services, having already seen use that year between Cardiff and Derby. Regarded as the final design of the so-called 'first generation' units, the four-car Swindon-built Inter-City DMUs probably offered the best travel experience for passengers in a multiple unit and it was a pity that they never seemed to find a lasting role during their twenty-odd years of service. The B4 and B5 bogies on which they rode were a new design at the time, later to provide decades of use under Mk1 and Mk2 rolling stock. When new, the corridor connection on the DMBS (Driving Motor Brake Second) had a yellow plastic cover, serving to make it one of the more visible trains on the network at the time. (Alec Swain N75-2)

Opposite: A close-up view of the nose of a Blue Pullman power car (W60092), taken in February 1967 at Old Oak Common, after the 'Manchester Pullman' service had gone over to electric haulage on the Euston route and the Midland Region's two diesel sets had transferred to the Western. In order to run these two six car sets as a single twelve car train on the busiest Bristol Pullman services, Motor Brake Firsts W60090/1/2/3 were equipped with unsightly Multiple Unit jumper cables and a standard screw coupling between their buffers. The three air horns were also repositioned (as seen here), though these seem to have had their baffle plates removed. Only the two ex-Midland sets ran in multiple; the remaining eight car sets were never able to couple up to them or with each other. Overall, the Western Region tried to make the best use of their Pullmans whereas the Midland always kept one of their sets as a spare, which was rather wasteful when you consider the investment that had been made in them. The arrival of better riding air-conditioned Mk 2 stock in the early 70s meant that the diesel Pullmans were no longer so appealing to travellers and were withdrawn en bloc in 1973. The loco-hauled Manchester Pullman continued in service for many years after, however. (Alec Swain V39-5)

Type 1 Diesels

Opposite: A north London scene from 1 September 1959 which is full of period interest: The photographer's vantage point is on the Old Oak Lane bridge in front of Willesden Junction station with English Electric Type 1 No. D8015 of 1D Devons Road (Bow) shed bringing a mixed freight round the curve from the Brent direction. The first twenty of this class of loco were initially allocated to Devons Road between 1957-58. To the far right will be noted a building with a large sign out front stating 'LMS Enquiry Office'. Over to the left is a signal box (thought to be Willesden No. 5) next to the main line with carriage sidings beyond and Acton Lane Power Station occupying the skyline beyond it. In the foreground are the DC electrified lines into the Low Level Junction station itself. The row of ten terraced houses seen above the crane in the yard remain today, as do some of the sidings to the rear of the train, but much of the site of the former goods yard is now occupied by a bus garage. (Nick Nicolson LN1586)

Above: Moving practically from one end of Britain to the other, on 22 April 1962 we find D8028 working a railtour in the rural setting of Lauriston where the station had closed to passengers in 1951. Lying on the very scenic Montrose to Inverbervie branch in Aberdeenshire, this station must have served an area for the sake of agricultural traffic, as few people lived near to it. After this date, the branch would see another four years of goods-only service before complete closure. As for the train itself, this was the 'Scottish Rambler'; a marathon four-day joint tour organised by the Branch Line Society and the Scottish area of the Stephenson Locomotive Society (according to the brilliant *'Six Bells Junction'* website). For the price of £7.75, it was billed as an opportunity for enthusiasts from all over the country to sample a wide range of Scottish lines in one visit – presumably they had to organise their own hotel stays in Glasgow, Inverness, Aberdeen and Perth. The tour involved the use of eleven different steam and diesel locomotives. (WAC Smith WS5925)

Opposite top: Nose-end first working of the EE Type 1s was awkward for footplate crews but more acceptable initially, bearing in mind that this situation was perhaps not so different to that of the steam locomotives they were already accustomed to. Kittybrewster-allocated D8029 heads a pick-up freight (which includes a Mk1 parcels coach next to the guard's van) from Aberdeen into Maud Junction sometime in the early 1960s. The photographer will probably have watched the train pick its way slowly down the hill in the distance and then across the fields to this station for its next call. This may have only been a small station but the 'WAY OUT' is clear enough and one very important facility here has its own illuminated sign saying 'BAR'. After a spot of shunting in the yard, it can be imagined that those involved would gladly have sought refreshment therein! The consumption of alcohol whilst on duty was acceptable in those days, not any more... (Sandy Murdoch SM386)

Opposite bottom: Now at the north end of the station, we see the same loco in the middle of shunting. The fact that four railway staff seem to be in attendance (driver, second man, shunter and guard), might give a clue as to why this sort of activity was costing BR too much when set against the revenue to be earned. Maud Junction served as an important railhead for the transport of cattle. Although there was no shed, there was a turntable of which the remnants can still be seen. Note that the platform has been constructed from the same kind of stone blocks that the station buildings seem to be made from; unsurprisingly, much of this stands to this day and a small railway museum has been established here, which is open from April to October. (Sandy Murdoch SM412)

Above: The British Thomson-Houston Type 1 design was influenced by the American 'road switcher', with its full-length engine hood. Industrial designers Allen-Bowden styled it, whereas the competing English Electric loco shape was the work of a team from London's Royal College of Art! According to David Lawrence's book *British Rail Designed 1948-97*, neat touches incorporated in the D8200 included a step in the roof at one end of the cab (to reduce the impression of bulk) and the grouping of ventilation grilles in a line above the cant rail. The running plate also had a curved underside. In the dying days of operation on the Framlingham branch (probably late 1964/ early 1965), D8220 is captured passing St Mary's church at Parham. This was a six-mile long line from Wickham Market Junction whose passenger services had ended back in 1952. A footpath to the church can be seen crossing the River Ore, via wicket gates on either side of the track. (Dr Ian Allen ICA D997)

Above: Next in the fleet, No. D8221 shunts an engineers' train in the snow-covered yard at Felixstowe Town in January 1970. Problems were being experienced with frozen points and various tools can be seen lying by the track in the right foreground. Before the direct line to the docks was reinstated, the Town station became very busy as a reversal point for the increasing number of liner trains that were beginning to serve the port. This was following industrial relations problems at the Port of Tilbury, which had led to transport firms seeking a nearby alternative. Felixstowe has prospered ever since! The station was unstaffed, yet was supporting an hourly train service to Ipswich whilst accommodating the freight train movements, at times occupying all four platforms and part of the disused goods yard. After the direct curve to the docks became available in May that year, facilities here were reduced to a single line. (Dr Ian Allen ICA D776)

Opposite: It always causes a bit of a smile to see new cars being transported by rail, even if the product being carried does end up being a competitor! This mixed train passing the box at Old Oak Junction has Mercedes and NSU Prinz cars from Germany on board, probably on their way from Parkestone Quay to an offloading terminal in West London. The date is 9 August 1963. In those days buying a car that was produced abroad was very much the exception. In the distance can be glimpsed the High Level signal box at Willesden Junction, though what an awkward stretch of track this must have been for the patroller with the conductor rail, return rail, check rail and point rodding all to contend with! Locomotive No. D8238 proved to be one of the shortest lived of its type: New to Finsbury Park depot in December 1960, it was to be withdrawn in the month following that of the last steam on BR. (Alec Swain O9-2)

Opposite top: Pictures of the NBL Type 1 in the D8400 series are ones often taken at Stratford depot (where they were all based for their entire life); less often of trains being worked out on the line. There was a reason for that! Apart from being unreliable, their performance generally compared poorly with that of the EE Type 1 and it is likely that, given the choice between the two on shed of a morning, drivers would pick a D8000 for the job in hand. On 30 April 1960, D8401 looks in good condition but with one equipment door slightly ajar, is it ready for the road? The first example of these ten pilot scheme locos to be withdrawn was D8404, scrapped in July 1968 before the end of steam on BR. The last had gone by the end of 1969. What would have become a class 16 had experienced less design input than the BTH version, instead being heavily based upon the LMS-conceived No. 10800: Seemingly covered in grills and grab handles, this wasn't a pretty locomotive. (Nick Nicolson LN3/2/3)

Opposite bottom: Wasn't it rather contradictory for BR to look for a single engine design for its standard Type 4, on the grounds that this helped to reduce maintenance costs, whilst choosing a 'standard' Type 1 that used two engines? One big advantage that the Clayton Type 1 had, of course was its vastly superior vision from the cab, compared to the others in the same power category – this wasn't enough to save it from oblivion, so poor was the performance of its horizontally mounted Paxman engines. The order for a hundred EE Type 1 replacements had gone in by the time D8616 (the final class member, with number unusually inserted on the buffer beam) was seen in Peterhead yard around 1966/ 67. Apart from the loco interest, one wonders what the gentleman in the suit, getting out of a Singer Vogue might be doing next to the old engine shed. Is he a manager on an inspection visit and wondering what the pile of rubbish is inside? The photographer (possibly accompanying him) was perched on the signal gantry guarding the station approach. By this time all passenger services had ceased; freight would follow in 1970. There has been some suggestion that the expansion of the town might yet lead to re-opening of the line from Dyce. However, that would be expensive, considering that the main Aberdeen to Inverness line with which it would connect is over 50 miles distant plus the old route is now the Formartine & Buchan Way cycle path. (Sandy Murdoch SM388)

Above: And so on to another unsuccessful small locomotive! Or was it? So many of the Swindon-built diesel-hydraulic 0-6-0s ended up working in industry, followed by preservation that you have to say that there wasn't a lot wrong with the design. It was a case of wrong place, wrong time with BR deliberately running down the sort of activity for which it was most appropriate. On 28 November 1964, having been in service for about a week, No. D9521 slows through the platform at Acton Main Line before being routed into the yard with its mixed rake of stock from Paddington Goods. This example of class 14 spent a good number of years with the National Coal Board at Ashington, in common with several others and can now be found at the Dean Forest Railway. (Alec Swain R26-1)

Type 2 Diesels

Above: The 24 July 1958 finds No. D5000, an early product of the Pilot Scheme plan, being brought for demonstration to the press at Marylebone. This terminus seemed to be a favourite for launch events as it was a relatively quiet station and centrally placed in London, near to BR HQ. D5000 was the first diesel-electric to emerge from one of BR's main works under the Modernisation Plan. The thin line around the centre of the loco was only applied to this example. (Alec Swain S92-1)

Opposite top: Two of the BR/ Sulzer Type 2 pilot scheme series, Nos. D5003 & D5009 prepare to head home as light engines after handing over a Margate to Derby train to Black 5 No. 45260 at Kensington Olympia. The date is 22 August 1959 and by this time, most of this first batch of twenty locos were hard at work on the Southern Region, based at Hither Green shed. These were never intended to stay there for long but were required to help bring about the end of steam under the Kent Coast electrification plan; once sufficient new Type 3 locos in the D6500 series were delivered, they would be returned to the London Midland Region. (Dick Riley RCR14179)

Opposite bottom: At Maud Junction on the Formartine & Buchan Line in Aberdeenshire, the second man of D5070 on a Peterhead-bound freight train is collecting the tablet manually with the signalman; the stands for the tablet exchange system, originally devised by GNSR engineer James Manson, can be seen either side of the track to enable this to be done for passenger trains passing at speed. The 1160hp BR/ Sulzer Type 2 was designated class 24 under TOPS. External design consultants had been unable to exert proper influence on the appearance of the BR Type 2 until half had been built. With untidy air intakes on the bodyside and other features presenting more of a maintenance headache than with the later class 25s, the 24s became early targets for withdrawal as freight traffic continued its decline through the 1970s. (Sandy Murdoch SM414)

Above: Construction of the 477 BR Type 2s was carried out at Derby, Crewe and Darlington, as well as in the private works of Beyer-Peacock at Gorton. D5094 was the first to emerge from Darlington sixty years ago on 12 January 1960, as seen here. It certainly looks like it was a big day for the workforce because it appears someone has arranged for a local beauty queen to attend and 'drive' the loco out of the building. Luckily it isn't raining, otherwise the lack of fitted windscreen wipers might have been a problem! (Photographer unknown)

Opposite top: On another unknown date around 1966, No. D5178 from the first of the uprated 1250hp batch of locomotives has the relatively easy task of powering a saloon around the York area. This six-wheel vehicle E900269E was built by the North Eastern as No. 41, an officer's inspection saloon with a balcony at one end. It looks as if it should have ended up on an allotment somewhere, or maybe as a pavilion for a small local cricket club but is believed to be in preservation now at the Alne Valley Railway. (Henry Finch)

Opposite bottom: Finally, BR was able to present the preferred version of its Sulzer-powered Type 2, as seen here in the case of D7544: With the connecting doors gone, a larger set of windscreens was possible and the side vents were now mostly tidied up at cantrail level. Side cab windows were of the sliding variety, as opposed to the more traditional droplight. The compulsory head code box on the roof was not something the designers could easily address, however. The date was April 30 1965 and the location, Marylebone Goods Yard, where an exhibition in conjunction with the 7th International Congress on Combustion Engines was reportedly being held. By the time the last of these class 25 locos were appearing in service, they were being turned out in BR's new blue livery with full yellow ends. Although they spent most of their lives working freight, their 90mph capability came in useful at times, particularly when called upon to double head certain longer distance Summer Saturday extras. (Alec Swain R94-4)

Opposite top: Photographer Eric Sawford was very much a recorder of steam motive power. However, he has cleverly captured four different types of diesel in one shot in this view at Kings Cross on 12 September 1959, together with an A4 Pacific. D6109 looks to be working an outer suburban service, whilst D5311 has just come up from the stop blocks; both would likely be meeting up again somewhere north of the border a few years later! On the station's stabling point can be seen a 'Baby Deltic' and an EE Type 4. Watching locos manoeuvring back and forth across the station throat, as they made their way to and from this facility, provided hours of entertainment for platform end enthusiasts up until the 1980s. (Eric Sawford ES4263)

Opposite bottom: No. D5308 passes through Alloa with a westbound train around 1966. The third coach is a Bulleid open third, recently transferred from the Southern Region; some were to last in service on the ER until around 1970. This relatively grand station had seen better days (the furthest platform bay had been lifted) though freight traffic, especially coal, was still very buoyant. Several industrial premises in the town were rail-served (including a brewery and glassworks), warranting the attention of a Dunfermline-based NBL 0-4-0 shunter No. D2718 around that period. When the route from Stirling was re-opened for passenger services in May 2008, the new station had to be placed beyond the bridge in the background as much of the original site had become occupied by a leisure centre. Only a single track remains through here. (Norris Forrest NF243-06)

Above: It was never supposed to be like this! The architects of the 1955 Modernisation Plan would doubtless have been horrified to think that modern diesel locomotives would need filling up with water in order to make steam, but that is how things transpired. Irish practice during dieselisation was to provide boiler facilities in separate coaches, rather than within the loco. The time when all passenger trains would become electrically heated was still decades away when this view of D5336 at Aberfeldy was recorded. The loco had just worked a short mixed train from Ballinluig Junction and would be ready to return there on the next service, once the water was attended to. One remnant of this branch, which was to be closed in 1965, is the Logierait Viaduct across the River Tay. This fine lattice ironwork structure passed to the local landowner when the railway had gone. Then, after being threatened with demolition, it was restored for limited use in 2001 as a community-owned road bridge. (Norris Forrest NF207-34)

Opposite top: Believed to be on 11 July 1964, 15A (Leicester)-based D5388 enters the down platform loop at the old Bromsgrove station on 2V72, an afternoon Birmingham New Street to Worcester Shrub Hill working. This all-stations stopping service would also have called at Blackwell and Stoke Works, two stations which were slated for closure by BR the following January, along with Bromsgrove, Barnt Green, Northfield, Bourneville and Selly Oak. The latter group were to survive after much local opposition but Blackwell and Stoke Works finally succumbed in early 1966. The Wagon Works in the background closed in October of 1964. Bromsgrove itself was to lose the down platform during re-alignment works in 1969, by which time only one train a day in each direction was calling there. Today's new station to the south of this location was opened in 2016, with four platforms and a passenger train service transformed to suit a town that has grown considerably since the 1960s. (Alec Swain Q9-6)

Opposite bottom: Brand new D5379 pauses at Oakley Junction, north of Bedford, with a driver training special returning to Cricklewood on 6 April 1962. The four-track Midland Main Line, with its double-posted telegraph poles can be seen on the right. No. D5379 was the first of these (eventually class 27s) to be allocated to the LMR's Midland Lines; also becoming one of the final few products to emerge from BRCW's Smethwick Works before that company withdrew from railway rolling stock production. The entire fleet of 1250hp Type 2s from their factory (69 in all) was delivered between July 1961 and November 1962, which was a pretty rapid output compared to what you might expect today. In 1938, Oakley Junction had been the scene of a head-on collision involving a down express that had got diverted onto the branch (after over-running signals), amid confusion during the shunting of an empty stock train that was already there. (Alec Swain L74-1)

This page: An unidentified pilot scheme series Brush Type 2 is seen on the approach to London's Liverpool Street station with an up express, passing the remnants of Bishopsgate Low Level, which had closed in 1916. These first diesels from the Loughborough workshops may have had a modest rating of only 1250hp, but they were put to work on fairly heavy duties from the off; it was soon clear that they struggled to outperform a class 5 rated steam loco in good order, such as a B1. However, footplate crews happily accustomed themselves to warm cabs and a comfortable seat, without having to worry about the level of water in the gauge glass or the quality of the coal in the tender. (Roy Vincent REV103-4)

Above: The 'Brush 2s' made East Anglia their home for more or less their entire career with BR. Locomotive No. D5572 found a certain degree of fame in 1966 when Messrs Tri-ang chose to use it as one of the few diesel models in their range, steam being obviously far more popular at the time. This view shows it propelling a BG and inspection saloon DE902260 near to Thorpeness, on the Aldeburgh branch. The milepost helpfully tells us that we are about a mile and a half beyond what is today the current end of line, at the Leiston nuclear flask loading pad. The loco lasted in service until May 2006 (as No 31154). DE902260 is remarkably still running on the network as the oldest vehicle in the rake of the 'Royal Scotsman' luxury touring train. (Dr Ian Allen ICA D1409)

Opposite top: No detail accompanied this photo of 5667 in the late 1960s, so we are indebted to the assistance of Andy Wallis in identifying it as Ryburgh, on the Wymondham to Wells line. It is inconceivable that an allotment would be allowed this close to an operational railway today; at the very least, the gentleman on the right would need to be clad in orange and be given a safety brief each time he wanted to water his carrots! After passenger services ended in 1964, this line had stayed open as far as Fakenham and remained so up to the early 1980s, thanks to buoyant freight traffic (particularly grain). The malting seen here has now expanded its site across the railway. And the locals must endure the sight and sound of the biggest trucks rumbling through their village, no doubt! (Dr Ian Allen ICA D1346)

Opposite bottom: Number D5668 pulls into Cavendish station with what was likely to have been a Summer Saturday Leicester to Clacton service, later to be re-routed via Bury St Edmunds and Ipswich upon closure of this line. Despite various operating economies, including the use of railbuses for a time, services between Colchester and Cambridge (via Sudbury) were discontinued at the close of 1966; local resistance had been insufficient to change the mind of Transport Minister, Barbara Castle. The station buildings were demolished soon after, even before the track was lifted. The photo was taken from the steps of the signal box, as the signalman waits to hand over the Tyer's tablet. In the Transport Treasury archive, there are several atmospheric images of Cavendish station which were captured by Paul Hocquard in its dying days, ranging from passengers waiting on the platform to Aylesbury Ducks feeding beside the signal box! (Dr Ian Allen ICA D414)

Above: Awaiting to be disposed of in the yard at the Brush Works, Loughborough is this cab mock-up, believed to be made of wood. Before assembly of the Brush Type 2 fleet began, this was used to get some feedback from railwaymen as to the suitability of the design. The headcode box on top of the cab was a later addition. Some fifty years later (in his capacity as a fleet engineer), the writer paid a visit here to view some modified Driving Van Trailers and sought permission to take photos of a couple of stored class 92s there – this was refused! We live in different times. (Alec Swain G45-1)

Opposite: The full restoration of this locomotive (at Bury) must be one of the most eagerly awaited in diesel preservation, even if the design was deemed a failure. In more hopeful times, Metro-Vick Co-Bo No. D5705 is shown at Kentish Town depot in September 1959. There is some graffiti on its side referring to Kettering, which may be less than complimentary! As Brian Haresnape wrote in the first part of his *'BR Fleet Survey'* series, 'Why was it, one now wonders, that such an odd-looking design also proved to be so troublesome; was it indeed the antithesis of *handsome is as handsome does*?' (Jim Flint FH1580)

Above: On 23 May 1963, D5711 and D5714 are shown being trialled on a Tunstead to Northwich stone train. The July issue of '*Modern Railways*' for that year reported tests on the ICI limestone hopper workings taking place over three days. Here on the third day two locos were used with 19 hoppers, which they managed but with some braking problems. In June, No. D5700 surprisingly was seen working the train alone on several occasions; earlier tests with EE Type 4s had been less successful with just 16 hopper wagons in the formation, damaged wheel tyres and brake blocks having been reported. With the relative unreliability of the Metro-Vicks now apparent, various attempts were being made to find a useful role for them. Keeping them on short distance work, from which they were unlikely to stray was one approach. It is unclear how long these particular trials continued; however, a single Sulzer Type 2 became the normal motive power on these trains in subsequent years. It would be interesting know why one gentleman in attendance (perhaps from Metro-Vick?) chose to wear a white lab coat. (Jim Flint FH2500)

Opposite top: D5902 picks its way out of 'The Cross' on 9 September 1959. In their early days, only Hitchin drivers were trained on the Baby Deltics, thus restricting them to duties on the southern section of the ECML. Once their reconditioning programme at Vulcan Foundry had been completed in 1965, their sphere of operations widened somewhat; one example was even seen visiting Skegness on a Summer Saturday. Note the steam loco stabled in the siding next to the tunnel entrance – small diesels made use of this facility too. (Eric Sawford ES4255)

Opposite bottom: D5903 applies the power to get what looks to be quite a heavy train of suburban stock away from the terminus at Kings Cross. The date was 29 June 1961. In common with their larger Type 5 relatives, the Baby Deltics emitted plenty of smoke on acceleration, something which must have been very unpleasant for commuters as their trains headed out through the several tunnels leaving London. The work carried out on their Napier power units between 1964-65 improved their reliability but not their tendency to produce thick smoke. The majority of this small fleet of ten locomotives were withdrawn in 1968-69, though two soldiered on until early 1971; their disappearance seemed to go without much comment in the railway press. Curiously, No. D5901 was to see further use in departmental service until 1976; one wonders why just one Sulzer Type 2 could not have been spared for this – perhaps the staff at Derby liked a challenge. (Nick Nicholson LN5-77-4)

Type 2 Diesels

Opposite top: On the subject of smoky exhausts, we have a contender in the shape of this NBL Type 2 (thought to be D6146) at Longside on the Peterhead branch, just as it has been given the road. Considering that the oncoming freight has seemingly only just entered the up loop (with tail lamp!), the signalman has worked quickly to get the passenger service on its way. Note the tablet exchange point opposite the box. Amongst a number of problems, these locos were prone to exhaust fires and the combination of the MAN power unit and GEC generator did not work well. Footplate crews soon grew to doubt their reliability, secondmen often coming to work in the expectation that they might well be shovelling coal again! (Sandy Murdoch SM035-12)

Opposite bottom: D6102 emerges from Hadley Wood Tunnel on a King's Cross-bound stopping service, headed by Gresley 'Quad-Art' set No. 83. These carriages, although quite basic inside, were of a design well-suited to the route they operated. Using articulated bogies helped to reduce rolling resistance and assist acceleration from frequent station stops, while their shorter length allowed them to fit the platforms on the Metropolitan Widened Lines to Moorgate. The date is 18 May 1959, which was shortly after the completion of the quadrification works along this stretch of the ECML. With the opening of the extra two tracks and accompanying new tunnel bores, the train is shown running on the up slow line. The new formation in the foreground became the down slow and down fast lines, respectively (note the 'DS10B' and 'DF10B' plates on the automatic signals). It is a pity that this route enhancement could not have been extended to encompass the Welwyn Viaduct and Tunnels – no doubt it was regarded as being too expensive back then; what has changed today? (Photographer unknown)

Above: Buchanan Street station in Glasgow is the setting for this platform end scene in mid-1966, a matter of weeks before the station was closed. One of the first re-engined NBL Bo-Bo type 2s (to become class 29 under TOPS), No. D6106, waits to leave on an express for Dundee. Apart from the first of these locos to be re-engined (with a Paxman 1350hp unit), the class 29s were distinct from the un-modified class 21s by having a four-character headcode panel; for some reason though, Scottish crews generally seemed reluctant to put up anything more than the class of train being worked. '*Modern Railways*' magazine reported at the time that in the August, this loco had taken over from two of the three A4 Pacifics which had remained in service for working the 3-hr Aberdeen services. All three were withdrawn by the end of September. An enthusiast (who seems to be carrying some sort of musical instrument in his bag) chats to the secondman, while to the right of shot someone is opening the door to their 'bothy' (an ex-LMS coach) and the station cat advances in hope! Buchanan House, British Rail's new Glasgow offices built on land that was formerly occupied by carriage sidings, can be seen under construction behind; it would open the following year. (Terry R Smith)

Opposite top: No. D6139 was not to be one of the lucky ones selected for a replacement engine at Inverurie Works. Instead it would succumb to withdrawal at the close of 1967, in common with many others. That date was some way off though when the loco was captured shunting the small yard at Mintlaw on 5 April 1965. Again, we appear to have four railway employees handling the task, which seems excessive. Note the NBL diamond worksplates at both ends of the locomotive. It is interesting that the Blue Pullmans also utilised the same MAN power unit that was fitted to the NBL Type 2 – perhaps the different duty cycle suited it better but the Pullmans certainly had their fair share of engine problems. (Sandy Murdoch SM521)

Opposite bottom: This shot, taken at J MacWilliam's scrapyard at Shettleston in May 1968, would seem to tell a story of the failure of the North British Locomotive Company. We see six locos that had been brand new barely eight years before, withdrawn within months of the last steam workings that ran in Scotland. In the foreground, No. D6151 has not even lasted long enough in service to be given a half-yellow warning panel, which suggests that it may have been put aside after a failure as early as 1963 and never worked again. D6144 behind it, also with worksplates and tablet catching apparatus removed, awaits a similar fate. One wonders how many of the men who built these engines, just a few miles away across the city of Glasgow, were aware of this and what their thoughts might have been. (WAC Smith WS9313)

Above: D6152 handles a northbound mixed consist of wagons, vans and coaches at Carmont (near Stonehaven) on a gloriously sunny day in the mid-1960s. A milk lorry is made to wait at the level crossing, just as it should be! (Paul Hocquard)

Above: No. D6305, one of the early batch of 1000hp type 2 diesel-hydraulics, has been caught by Dick Riley's camera beside the steam shed at Laira (Plymouth) on 9 July 1961. It is in the company of No. D6310, which was from the production 1100hp rated batch. Several detail differences can be noted, from the arrangement of grilles on the bodyside to the positioning of the windscreen wipers. One characteristic of many of the North British diesels produced at the time was their spoked wheels; rather anachronistic in appearance, they did serve to reduce the amount of unsprung weight in the bogies and were said to have promoted a smoother ride for the footplate staff! Although the D63xx series was seen as the hydraulic equivalent of the D61xx diesel-electrics, the latter were significantly longer due to having to accommodate a generator. They also didn't use the Commonwealth type bogie of the diesel-electric. The hydraulics officially outlasted them in service, it should be said! (Dick Riley RCR16049)

Opposite top: Recently delivered Nos. D6307 & D6306 are seen just after arrival at Paddington, having worked the 7.5am from Cheltenham Spa on 16 October 1959. The December issue of *'Trains Illustrated'* magazine reported that these two were rostered to that service on the 7, 9, 12, 14 and 16 of October and returning each time on the Kensington to Whitland milk empties, as far as Swindon. This seemed to be a regular pattern for the running-in of new diesels on the Western Region, in the early days at least, probably as expertise for correcting any faults was mostly at Swindon. One of the advantages of the Type 2 was thought to be the fact that they could be easily doubled up to become the equivalent (albeit an expensive one) of a single Type 4. This flexibility was fine for duties in Devon and Cornwall but the low 75mph maximum speed of the D6300s would mean that sights such as this would always be a rarity. (Nick Nicolson LN2/34/1)

Opposite bottom: In that same week, on 13 October 1959, No. D6309 is caught scuttling through Preston station en route from Glasgow to Swindon, on delivery from the manufacturer. It would enter service at Laira in January 1960. Both these and the diesel-electric versions of the NBL Type 2 unusually employed vertically hinged headcode discs and on what was a very cluttered looking front end for a brand new locomotive. It would appear that somebody hasn't secured the hatch to the boiler water tank filler. (Arnold Battson)

More detail differences are evident on No. D6329 as it rests between duties at its home depot of Newton Abbot shed (83A) on 28 June 1966: Almost flush-fitting headcode boxes have been fitted either side of connecting doors that fold, as well as being hinged. Grab handles have been repositioned and the twin vents above the windscreens have gone. With the disappearance of many of the branch line and pick up goods duties they were ideal for, some of the D6300s gravitated to working empty stock in and out of Paddington. In the end, however much these TOPS class 22s might have settled down in reliability terms, their workload was diminishing wherever they went and was easily covered by other fleets of diesels. (Alec Swain U64-5)

Type 3 Diesels

In the last few months of passenger services on the Isle of Grain, in place of the Wainwright H class tank engines normally turned out, were occasional substitutions by BRCW Type 3 diesels. The servicing of steam at Gillingham depot had finished in June 1960, so it became convenient for some of the diesels that were now dominant on local freight to work some of the Allhallows branch passenger trains. The result was the slightly incongruous sight of a new diesel locomotive coupled to two examples of ex-LBSC or ex-LSW non-corridor stock, such as here at Sharnal Street with No. D6518 on a Gravesend to Allhallows train during 1961. There is little sign of any activity here, other than a couple of water cans on the up platform; note also the lamp hut made of corrugated iron and built clear of the station building, due to the fire risk. Branch passenger trains ended in the December when the line assumed more importance as a freight artery, serving the Grain refinery and cement works. (Dave Clark)

Opposite top: Moving towards the other end of the decade (and almost to the other side of the Southern Region), we have D6530 taking a lengthy passenger train along the Swanage branch on 7 August 1965. A plume of steam may be observed rising from the area of Corfe Castle station so it's possible that this train has just passed an up working. The locomotive was reported as being the first of its class to receive small yellow warning panels in 1962 and was unique in having ones with rounded top corners. Many others didn't receive theirs until 1966, by which time the blue livery with full yellow ends was starting to be applied. The rooftop cooling fan shows that this is the No.1 end of the loco. (Peter Gray)

Opposite bottom: The Cromptons, as they became known by enthusiasts, worked away from their home depots from quite early in their careers. There were the celebrated Cliffe to Uddingston cement trains (with locos normally changed at York), and also several oil tanker train diagrams emanating from the Fawley refinery which required Western Region crews to be trained upon them. D6583 is seen passing the yard of Worcester Works on 1 June 1963 with oil tankers returning from Bromford Bridge; the train would be routed onwards via Oxford and Didcot and is using the goods avoiding lines, which diverged from the main line at Tunnel Junction (in the background) and went round the side of Shrub Hill station. In the January, No. D6518 had become the first diesel to be based in the Worcester area in order for the necessary crew-training to be carried out. It saw use on a variety of local passenger services as a result. (Dick Riley RCR17155)

Above: The story of the transition from steam to diesel traction in the Stratford depot district is superbly related in Dick Hardy's book '*Railways in the Blood'*. He presided over the transformation of one of the country's largest installations, from a steam shed to a diesel depot. This involved the reskilling of a small army of employees; the retraining of boilermakers to electricians, being one example. English Electric Type 3 D6708 sits alongside Brush Type 2 D5540 on 17 February 1962. These two mixed-traffic types formed the backbone of East Anglia's motive power for thirty years, practically. Drivers tended to prefer the latter for freight duties, finding them slightly more sure-footed – a bit surprising when you consider that only four axles were driven, as opposed to six on the Type 3. Despite ceding an advantage of 250hp to their EE Type 4 cousins though, the future class 37s performed almost as equals to them on passenger services. (Nick Nicolson LN6/49/1)

Opposite: Two English Electric Type 3 diesels (with D6725 leading) thunder over the crossover at Murrow West, heading a lengthy mixed freight train northwards. The main feature here was (and still is) the signal box. After a major collision between two freight trains had occurred on the crossing during the war, demolishing the original structure, this modern looking replacement opened in 1950. Today, it has been added to and extended into an interesting dwelling whilst the railway (sadly) has completely disappeared. By the time of the photograph (in the mid 1960s), the Midland & Great Northern line had been closed as a through route since 1959. Its single track remained at this location until 1966 in order for some residual freight traffic to continue to serve a brickworks at Eye, as well as the yard at Wisbech; a new north curve (behind the photographer) had been provided for trains to arrive via the main GN & GE Joint line. (Dr Ian Allen ICA D511)

Above: There's a match on at Wembley (an England versus Wales Schools Soccer International) so D6798 has been tasked with working the 1X56 special service from Sheffield Victoria. It is seen being routed into the up platform at Gerrards Cross on 27 April 1963, having worked south via the Great Central. There doesn't appear to be anyone waiting on the platform to join so it is possible the train was being looped, allowing an express service to overtake it, before proceeding onwards to Wembley Hill. The posters displayed on the station are for Lowe's Carta Carna with Meat (dog food), Nine Elms drinks and 'Drinka Springtime Pinta' (milk). (Alec Swain N41/1)

Opposite top: We don't have a date for this scene taken at Kemble station, though it is believed to be some time in the autumn of 1961, considering the immaculate condition of what was likely to have been a new locomotive. The weather is probably warm, judging by the open windows and the fact that people seem happy to stand and watch proceedings – perhaps the presence of a photographer is also enough to create interest! The branch railbus (one of the four from A C Cars Ltd of Thames Ditton) to Cirencester Town appears to have caught the attention of the driver on Hymek D7004, as it calls with the 2.40pm Gloucester Central to Swindon stopping service. After overhaul in 1966, this particular loco was to be given the unusual livery of all-over blue with half-yellow warning panels. (David Horne)

Opposite bottom: On 3 August 1965, D7009 has arrived in the through platform at Severn Beach while a DMU waits in the bay before forming a service to Bristol Temple Meads. Only the bay platform remains in use today. Passenger services over the loop line to Pilning Low Level had finished the previous year; what train the Hymek is working is unknown but is possibly just empty stock being routed away from the busy main line through Filton. Before complete closure of the loop in 1968, redundant wagons were stored beyond Ableton Lane Crossing in the background. Note the electric cabling (with a support wire) running between the station lights; this seemed to be a feature of railway stations in those days. (Alec Swain S95-2)

Above: It is well known that the Hymek diesel-hydraulics ran tests from Beyer-Peacock's Gorton plant in Manchester, across the Peak District (via Miller's Dale) to Derby Midland; not that many did so whilst still in undercoat! On 7 March 1962, D7028 has clearly run round it's rake of empty stock and is being prepared for the return journey; note the white overalled technician in the rear cab and that a worksplate has yet to be fixed below the cabside numbers (which appear to be painted in undercoat too!). The writer was particularly interested to come across this image because D7028 was the only one of the class which he managed to see in service, as a young spotter in 1974. (Alec Swain L55-1)

Opposite: Right up to the end of through working on the Great Central, there was interest to be found there on the motive power front. This view shows No. D7052 with the 6.40pm York to Swindon, calling at Leicester Central on 20 August 1966. New Hymeks had often been delivered to the Western Region using this route as far as Woodford Halse and then across to Banbury, via a link which could have proved useful on the network today, had it been safeguarded. The paucity of cross-country lines, causing so many journeys to become focused on London, is one factor which has hindered the possibility of the railways shouldering more of the transport burden in southern Britain. (Mike Mitchell MM3268)

Above: We end this chapter with another long-lamented closure, the line from Barnstaple Junction to Ilfracombe. D7095 is viewed from the road bridge at Barnstaple as it crosses the curved railway bridge over the River Taw with an up train on 20 July 1964 - the summer in which diesels assumed control from steam over that route. Although the last services ran in 1970, the final train to cross the bridge was believed to be an inspection special in 1975. Demolition came in 1977. This view emphasises how close the driver sat to the front on this design of locomotive. For some drivers, who had spent much of their footplate career with a large boiler between them and the line ahead, the switch to this sort of situation (with just a windscreen) was too much to accept; they didn't like the thought of having to drive like this at 80-90mph and opted for work in the slower DMU links. (R C Riley RCR17671)

Type 4 Diesels

Above: It was the first ten units of the Derby/Sulzer Type 4 series which gave rise to their overall nickname of 'Peaks', despite the fact that those of the rest of the 193 locos which were named had a regimental theme to them! Here we have No. D10 'Tryfan' apparently being reversed on one of the Crewe Independent lines on 6 July 1961. On 18 March that same year, D10 had been brought to St Pancras for an inspection by the then Minister of Transport Ernest Marples (remember him?) before it worked the 2.25pm train to Manchester. That was about as glamorous as things got for these Pilot Scheme (later class 44) Peaks as a few years later, all ten were transferred to Toton depot and spent most of their time on coal trains. Their 2300hp power units came from Sulzer's Winterthur Works – later ones were built under licence by Vickers Armstrong at Barrow-in-Furness – and the Crompton Parkinson generator fitted to them was said to be the biggest of its kind in Europe. (Alec Swain K65-3)

Opposite top: One of the more powerful 2500hp series 'Peaks', No. D24 arrives at Barrhead with the four coach 5.3pm Glasgow St Enoch to Kilmarnock on 14 July 1961. This loco had arrived at Corkerhill depot for crew training about two months before following an initial spell at Derby, where it had been built. The figure visible in the centre cab window suggests that some familiarisation is taking place, before these type 4s are let loose on more important duties. The gangway doors on the front of a 'Peak' usually denoted one of the D1-D10 batch but the first five of the Derby-built 2500hp locos were also equipped with them. This gave rise to the positioning of the two route indicator boxes at either side, of course, and that trend was continued for a short time (both on Derby and Crewe-built examples), even after the gangway doors were discontinued. (WAC Smith WS5562)

Opposite bottom: A Holbeck (55A) based No. D30 swings into Mangotsfield Junction station with what is probably a Derby to Bristol working in around 1963/ 64. This was the last of the Derby batch of locos fitted with the 'split boxes'. Mangotsfield was on the Midland Railway's route into Bristol, part of a network of that company's lines to the east of the city which were largely abandoned after 1969. The station itself was closed in 1966 but through trains continued to pass until the decision was made to concentrate traffic on the Filton route, via the soon-to-be opened Bristol Parkway. Over to the right is the Carson's Chocolate factory which sat inside a railway triangle. Photographer and artist George Heiron has captured the train perfectly against this backdrop, surrounding it with railway signage and a cyclist who is looking at the main subject, not the photographer! Today incidentally it is cycle routes which converge here, though one wonders whether the city wouldn't be better served by a tram system that uses these former railway corridors. (George Heiron)

Opposite: The 30 May 1961 finds D105 freshly out of the paint shop at Crewe Works, where 88 of what were to become the class 45s were constructed. The original plan was for only 70 to be built there but D50 to D67 were switched to Crewe and appeared after D68 to D137. In somewhat similar fashion, an order of five 'Western' diesel-hydraulics was also switched to Crewe from Swindon and the latter's production line was beginning just as that of the Peaks was winding down. D105 was one of the last to be given the split box headcodes; subsequent fitment saw these two panels fitted next to each other centrally and almost flush with the bodywork and that trend continued into the batch equipped with Brush traction equipment (to be class 46). The final style was a single central four-character headcode. (Alec Swain K42-3)

Above: D139 was the second of the 56 Peaks fitted with Brush electrical equipment. Seen at Turvey on 8 November 1961, during driver training on the Bedford to Northampton line, the locomotive is in spotless condition which allows easier study of the front-end detail, from its horizontally floating front axle (with no external axlebox) right down to the chains used to tie up some of the pipework. These were very heavy locos, turning the scales in the region of 138 tons. At this time of course, footplate crews would still dress as they had always done, in overalls that were appropriate for the firing and driving of a steam locomotive. This group seems to be in a relaxed mood as they pose for their colleague to record the moment on film. Shortly afterwards in March 1962, Turvey station would close to passengers and the route from Oakley Junction (at the Bedford end) closed entirely in 1964. (Alec Swain L30-5)

Above: Back to the Bristol area and we find a 'Peak' about to roar past the box at Westerleigh North whilst powering a train of passenger and postal stock northwards one summer's evening. The yard here was a wartime construction, built to serve Bristol but at a distance from it in order to help mitigate the chance of enemy bombing taking out the capacity of the whole city. The signalling seems to be a strange mix of Western and Midland: Upper quadrant semaphores and Western-type point rodding can be seen. The only railway presence left here today is a small civil engineer's facility and the Murco fuel terminal situated in the right distant background. One of Bristol's waste transfer depots was here too but has been unused since 2001. The chimney that is also visible belonged to the Parkfield Colliery (closed before the war) but which remains to this day. (George Heiron)

Opposite: First of its class, No. D200 is seen heading a Lowestoft bound summer Saturday service from Liverpool Street (via the East Suffolk route) at Oulton Broad South in 1961. The Stratford-based English Electric Type 4s were normally confined to the main line to Norwich at that stage, though clearly there was scope for one to be available for this duty. The train is swinging over the junction with the Kirkley Goods branch to Lowestoft South Side (closed around 1970). The junction signal box was just out of shot to the right of this view and the branch itself became single track immediately behind the photographer. The purpose of the building to the left is unclear but should a goods train of any size try to leave the branch out of control, the switch setting suggests there might not be much left of it, one suspects! Note the pipe suspended from the side of the road bridge and the small signal arm applying to traffic going on to the branch. (Dr Ian Allen ICA D1539)

Alec Swain served as shedmaster at Willesden during the transition from steam to modern traction and often had his camera ready to record all sorts of events taking place on his watch. Here we see EE Type 4 No. D207 being used for some track testing on 23 March 1959 at a spot known as Twyford Abbey Sidings. This area was at the west end of Brent Sidings, roughly opposite where the Princess Royal mail sorting depot is today, though now completely redeveloped. Although Camden depot would shortly receive an allocation of this type for working out of Euston, D207 however was then based at Hornsey; it seems that it had been borrowed to check the action of the 1Co-Co1 bogie when passing over a diamond crossover.

Although this isn't clearly visible, the huddle of Homburg-hatted engineers are looking closely at it while the loco crew await further instructions. Alec took photos of the crossover (specially inserted into the single track) afterwards and clear marks had been left by the loco's wheels, suggesting that there was a problem. This may go some way to explaining why the civil engineer imposed a short restriction on the use of EE Type 4s on the London Midland and they were thus confined to working Euston to Bletchley stopping services for a time. They would also suffer from cracks to their bogies throughout their BR service.
(Alec Swain E63-5)

One of the up stopping services mentioned approaches Berkhamsted on a sunny day in August 1959. EE Type 4 D210 was the first of its class to be allocated to the London Midland Region, after the first ten had gone to the Eastern. Note the nose end ladder that was fitted to a number of the earlier built examples, intended to facilitate access to the hatches on top of the nose, as well as the cab windows – they were quickly removed when the dangers to staff using them underneath overhead wires were properly realised. The change over from steam to diesel traction on the southern section of the West Coast Main Line would take several years to complete; steam would be working long distance services out of Euston more than three years after this picture was taken. The Scammell trailer on the right shows that Berkhamsted still looked to the railway for some of its general freight delivery, as well as the coal supplies that almost every town relied upon back then. The Clean Air Act of 1956 arguably marked the beginning of the end of widespread domestic coal consumption. However, winter smogs were to affect London and other cities well into the 1960s; another reason for the ending of steam traction, of course. (Jim Harbart FH1594)

Above: A substantial mixed freight train heads steadily northwards past the lineside TPO apparatus at Walton behind No. D237 on 6 September 1962. In the same month, the last of this class was released to traffic but a more advanced design of diesel-electric would also be making its debut in the shape of the Brush/Sulzer D1500. The coming of modern traction demanded development in the capabilities of the infrastructure, as well as rolling stock generally. In this view we can see various kinds of track, from the traditional bullhead rail upon wooden sleepers to flat bottom rail fixed with two different types of rail spike. A long-welded section of rail also appears to be sat in the six foot alongside the train, possibly in expectation of being used on one of the fast lines at some point. The faster speeds attained by diesel-hauled freight trains brought to light the shortcomings of the traditional short-wheelbase wagon. During the 1960s, there were many derailments resulting from broken axles, cyclic top and hunting. Higher axle loads also demanded the use of concrete sleepers and an even heavier section of rail to address the risk of rail breakages. Long-welded rail would help to reduce maintenance, as well as rolling stock running costs. No more would you see a man hammering wooden keys back into the rail chair on the main lines. (Eric Sawford ES4524)

Opposite top: By 1967, BR had acquired almost its full complement of Type 4 diesels in the 2500 – 2750hp power range. Lesser powered units that had come into service earlier in the Modernisation Plan could now be demoted to lesser duties such as we see here. One of the twenty class 40s built with split box headcodes either side of the gangway doors, No. D335 finds itself deep in the Leicestershire countryside at Shackerstone, working a southbound class 8 train of loaded coal wagons on 11 September 1967. A freight-only route by this stage, the Ashby to Nuneaton line would be closed completely two years later. Gratifyingly today, the buildings and substantial footbridge survive in use by the Battlefield Line, together with two tracks between the platforms. Although not perhaps in the 'big league' of preserved railways, the line has its own distinct appeal and the writer recommends anyone to make a visit there. The station building on the left now contains a museum with a remarkable collection of railway artefacts; train drivers have a tendency to park up in front of the buffet to grab refreshments! (Mike Mitchell MM3468)

This page, bottom: While the Great Central route was losing its principal passenger services, it was still proving useful for special trains that were run for the benefit of sports fans visiting Wembley from the East Midlands, Yorkshire or Humberside. These would usually call at Wembley Hill station, which is a short walk from the stadium. On 9 May 1964, several trains came down from Hull for the Rugby League Challenge Cup Final (between Hull KR and Widnes) but were reported as having run into Marylebone (via Amersham). This was possibly due to rebuilding work going on at Wembley Central, putting extra pressure on Wembley Hill. Whereas in previous years many specials had been steam hauled, this time those coming from Hull were English Electric powered: type 3s seen were Nos. D6732/ 39/ 40/ 53/ 79 & D6803 plus this with York-based D354. The location is the south end of Woodford Halse station, still comparatively busy (considering that complete closure was only two years or so away) with a 'Hall' and a V2 stood by as it passes. An RCTS special from Nottingham Victoria headed by 46251 'City of Nottingham' had also worked through that morning, which might explain the extra interest at the lineside. The driver sports a flat cap and seems keen to be seen by the camera – perhaps he'd been signal checked as well. This may also have been the last time that Wembley-bound specials used the London extension of the GC in quantity, many fans having to switch to using road coaches on the parallel M1 in the years following – was that progress? (George Smith GS2-40-2)

Above: This photograph shows a scene rarely captured at the time, namely a new engine fresh from the works of the North British Locomotive Company of Glasgow. Unfortunately, there are no notes to accompany a clutch of similar images taken of diesel-hydraulic Type 4 D603 'Conquest'. Entering service on the Western Region in November 1958, its spotless state suggests it hasn't been in traffic yet, though the loco is recorded as having returned to NBL in early 1959 for further attention. However, we do know the location is Kingsknowe (in the Edinburgh suburbs) and judging by the group in the front cab plus the open rear cab door, it looks as if the train has come to a halt. Could it be that the photographer has been riding with them? Either way, the train is blocking a road level crossing here and it can be assumed that the signalman won't be comfortable with that! In November 1968, D603 was scrapped. (Photographer unknown)

Opposite top: This is not a particularly happy scene. We have a practically brand-new locomotive already out of traffic … and one of its successors can be seen under construction in the background. D602 'Bulldog' sits in Swindon Works on 3 May 1959 and its relative cleanliness alone would suggest that it hasn't been in traffic for long. The basket of parts in the foreground and the removed section of roofing points to engine trouble; indeed, records show that it was making an unscheduled visit that lasted for a month. The Pilot Scheme D600 series of 'Warships' only saw use on long distance passenger work up until 1963, by which time it was clear they couldn't be used to speed up services beyond what was possible with ex-GW 'Castles' and 'Kings'. Being only five units, it made sense to concentrate them on a limited area for crewing purposes and they saw use mostly on freight and secondary passenger services in Cornwall, based at Laira. (Arnold Battson)

Right: Almost eight years later in March 1967, we encounter the same locomotive (D602) at Laira entering its last few months of service with BR. It's fair to say that within that comparatively short space of time, there had been enormous change on the network and a number of lessons learned with diesel traction in general. As far as the Western Region was concerned, the choice of diesel-hydraulic traction had not been a failure but was to be brought to an end, chiefly to reduce the costs of keeping spares and maintaining expertise for a 'niche' product. The closure of many lines and vast reduction in freight traffic across the network was about to release diesel-electric locos in all power categories, enough to replace the hydraulics in their entirety eventually. (Alec Swain V51-6)

Opposite top: 2000hp rated Type 4 'Warship' D801 'Vanguard' comes off the Royal Albert Bridge at Saltash, working the 'Cornish Riviera Express' in 1959. The background looks rather empty without the road suspension bridge, the construction of which was imminent at the time. It is suspected that the man stood by is likely to be the fireman of the Plymouth to Saltash shuttle service, as he seems to have cotton waste in his hand. Perhaps he is wondering when he will get to 'enjoy' the new form of traction, about to sweep steam away from the area over those next three years. The hand exchange of the key token without the usual hoop was common practice with diesel working. With plenty of space behind a steam locomotive's footplate, the hooped token would have somewhere to swing if this handover happened at speed. There may have been some damage caused in the case of a diesel. Note the Great Western designed ATC ramp in the four foot of the up line. (Alan Robey)

Opposite bottom: Passing Southall Shed at speed, D804 'Avenger' heads the 1.30pm Paddington to Plymouth train on 21 February 1960 - and speed was what this particular loco was known for in its early days, on one occasion being recorded at over 100mph. The train consists mostly of BR Mk1 coaches with a couple of ex-Great Western catering vehicles inserted. Another GW designed vehicle, namely a diesel railcar, can be seen behind the locomotive and parked adjacent to a water softening plant. A BR parcel unit (later to be a class 128) is just visible, together with a selection of tank engines at the shed itself. Not long afterwards, it was at this location that a group of teenage enthusiasts first got together to discuss buying a tank engine and auto-trailer from BR, leading to the formation of the Great Western Society and later the Didcot Railway Centre. (Brian Wadey)

Above: A landslip on the Berks & Hants near Lavington in August 1961 led to a number of interesting diversions, particularly on two busy Saturdays. Here, a relatively new D846 'Steadfast' approaches Basingstoke with an up West of England working. Although 'Warships' were later to become a familiar sight, in 1961 any diesel would have been uncommon on this route and one suspects that the individuals leaning from the first coach are more than aware of that! 'Trains Illustrated' magazine reported that on 26 August, another NBL 'Warship' D852 had been noted on the diverted 9.20am St Ives to Paddington (one of five trains sent over the former Southern route to Plymouth) and that the following Saturday had seen similar activity. Another feature to point out is the mix of upper and lower quadrant semaphore signals here. The train has clearly just passed some upper quadrants but the gantry on the left consists of the lower type, ex-LSWR Westinghouse low pressure pneumatic ones, to be precise. Operated by compressed air, the lack of heavy cabling to them can be detected. (Ken Coursey C424)

Above: In a scene recorded nearly sixty years ago beside the main line at Royal Oak, BR-built Warship No. D811 'Daring' brings the twelve coaches of train 'A41', the up 'Mayflower', into the capital on Saturday 27 August 1960. This service was the 08.30 from Plymouth, due into Paddington at 13.40 (13.25 on weekdays) and conveying a portion from Kingswear; it had been introduced into the timetable back in 1957. Note the joint between bullhead and flat-bottomed rail in the right foreground - this required a junction fishplate to keep a properly level railhead across the joint. Moving to the background, the Lord Hills Bridge still carries traffic today but many of the buildings beyond were not to survive the construction of the A40 Westway. With increasing train speeds and heightened safety concerns, it was inevitable that lineside photography on the national system would become prohibited. Together with the loss of industry-employed photographic teams, this means that far fewer images of this type have come to be recorded. Despite the improvements in photographic equipment, what breadth of archive will there be to study sixty years hence? (R C Riley RCR15311)

Opposite top: The 'Westerns' did not exactly cover themselves in glory during their first years in service. It's not known why D1004 'Western Crusader', then only a few weeks into service, needed front-end assistance from 'County' class 4-6-0 1019 'County of Merioneth' on 8 June 1962. However, the train has just passed Aller Junction, heading for Dainton Bank, therefore it is possible that one of its two Maybach engines is malfunctioning and the pilot engine has been attached at Newton Abbot to assist it as far as Plymouth (train 1V95 having originated at Manchester). The 'County' was to be withdrawn from service shortly afterwards. (Peter Gray).

Opposite bottom: D1006 sits outside Swindon Works 'A' shop on 24 June 1962, as many locomotives did after construction or overhaul, though not many were captured on film in undercoat, without name and number plates. It was noted in the railway press at the time that Crewe Works made quicker progress in building their allocated batch than Swindon and did it cheaper too. Over the years, some claimed that they could tell a Crewe-built Western apart from a Swindon one by looking at the finish of the bodywork; presumably the parochial ones would have it that the latter were of a better standard? Today, in preservation, we have four preserved examples from Swindon and three from Crewe. D1006 itself became one of the first of the class to receive standard BR blue livery in early 1967. (Stephen Hoather)

Above: A previous title in the Transport Treasury series had stated that photographer R C Riley did not seem to have photographed any 'Western' diesels. But here is one! D1019 'Western Challenger' rolls past Neasden North box, having brought the empty stock of '1X63' into the sidings there on 25 May 1963. The occasion for which this train and others ran was the FA Cup Final between Manchester Utd and Leicester City at Wembley, arranged later than normal that year because of the disruption caused to the football programme by the severe and prolonged winter weather. The train itself probably worked to Wembley Hill from the Chester area for the benefit of United supporters. The number of crewmen in the cab would suggest that the opportunity was also being taken to carry out some crew training. The delivery of the Westerns was rather protracted, due partly to the slow supply of components to the workshops, so training had to be done on service trains. By the time the last of the fleet was being delivered, plans were already being made to replace them with Brush Type 4s on the 'Northern' route out of Paddington. D1019 is only a few weeks old but already the windscreen wiper on the secondman's side has gone missing. (R C Riley RCR17105)

Opposite bottom: Here we are inside the engine room of a 'Western' in 1966, after it has been involved in a minor collision. The incident has caused the transmission to become inoperable from the driver's desk, so recourse is being made to free the mechanism manually. Alec Swain's colleague (dressed in an early style of driver's jacket) is inside the cooler group between the radiator elements, standing above one of the transmissions. By lifting one of the hinged metal flaps, he has gained access to the transmission control levers which can be used to manually select the direction of travel in order to help move the locomotive. In his book *'Diesels – a Driver's Reminiscences',* Colin Jacks wrote about training on the type at Tyseley shed. He highlighted the way in which operation of the train heating boiler was taught during running and in a very confined space; the use of hand gestures apparently the only way to communicate whilst crouched between two Maybach engines at full chat! When the class 52s were upgraded with the fitment of air braking, the engine room became even more cluttered. With thanks to the 'Western Research Society' who provided detail for this description. (Alec Swain V13-6)

Above: George Heiron clearly enjoyed visiting Badminton on the South Wales main line, whether it was to see 'Britannia' hauled expresses thundering through this wayside station on a fine summer's day or to experiment with night photography in the middle of winter. His activities would on occasion cause a degree of consternation amongst the station staff when they observed him standing in deep snow on the cutting side with his camera on a tripod! We may wonder what the driver of D1037 'Western Empress' is thinking here as he waits for the right-away towards Swindon with an up express, probably from South Wales in the 1963-65 period. Hopefully he wasn't looking at the flash gun when George fired it at his loco! (George Heiron)

Above: D1054 'Western Governor' sits in the yard at Crewe Works, well chocked and set up for testing of its steam heating equipment. The train heating boiler was the source of trouble for many diesels in their early years and a number of Westerns saw service on the Paddington-Birmingham-Birkenhead route with a steam loco coupled inside, particularly during the harsh winter of 1962-63. D1054's first allocation was to Cardiff Canton in March 1963 where it would help to relieve the hard-pressed Hymeks from some of the heavier South Wales express train duties. As with Laira depot, Cardiff Canton was opened to diesel maintenance in a progressive manner, with some work being shared with Landore at Swansea. The 1X97 headcode refers to a test run that Crewe-built 'Westerns' sometimes made to Chester and back. (Alan Cottrell)

Opposite top: In 1962, BR was assessing three prototype machines with a view to selecting one that would become its preferred second-generation Type 4. These were the 2800hp Brush 'Falcon', the 2750hp BRCW 'Lion' and the 2700hp English Electric DP2. Almost repeating the saga of a few years earlier, BR decided it couldn't afford to wait to see the full results of trials so went ahead and chose Brush to build it. With a design that owed a lot to that of 'Falcon' and using the power unit which BRCW had chosen for 'Lion' (which had taken too long to appear), they went straight into production with the D1500. To EE's apparent disadvantage, it had also been decided that all future locomotive designs would be flat-fronted. Meanwhile bereft of a potentially bulk order, BRCW went into liquidation. D1500 is seen arriving light engine from Derby in the shed yard at Cricklewood on 27 September 1962 (where Alec Swain was expecting it), a shining example of modernity in a clearly steam-era setting. The next few locos to come off the production line at Loughborough had builder's plates attached below the cabside number. The first twenty Finsbury Park based machines (fitted with electric train heating equipment from new) rarely left the ECML for twenty years, putting in huge mileages as they played second fiddle to the 'Deltics'. (Alec Swain M56-1)

Opposite bottom: Wherever diesels were stabled, the ground would always be stained with oil or be thick with black grease. Although not as bad as with steam, where lubrication of the engine was done on a 'total loss' basis, those locomotives that were constructed in the 1950s and 60s would always leak oil. If fresh ballast was dropped into the four foot of any busy railway, it was only a matter of months before a dark stain began to appear down the middle of it. Britain's railways were undoubtedly one of the worst polluting industries – in later years, the earth around some closed railway installations would have to be dug up and treated before redevelopment was permitted. Brush Type 4 D1677 stands outside Gloucester Horton Road shed on 27 October 1965; this was before it had received the name 'Thor', when the original recipient D1671 had been written off that December in the Bridgend accident. During the 1970s, when the Western Region still retained those class 47s which it had named, the writer recalls carefully entering the name 'George Jackson Churchward' into his notebook – surely one of the longest nameplates to appear on the side of a loco in this country! (Eric Sawford ES5679)

Above: In a photo that was probably taken around the middle of 1964, we find two recently introduced Brush Type 4s at the Paddington stopblocks. Even by this time, it was clear that the writing was on the wall for the Western Region's diesel-hydraulic fleet. D1720 was allocated to Bristol Bath Road and D1733 to Old Oak Common, so would have been sharing duties on the main lines to Bristol and South Wales with the 'Warships' and 'Westerns'. The 'V' headcode on D1733, which had been selected from new to trial BR's future standard blue livery, points to it having come down from Birmingham Snow Hill on a working originating at Birkenhead or Wolverhampton. Other things of note in the picture are the large quantities of mailbags and parcels trolleys cluttering up the platforms, the notices announcing the Bristol and South Wales Pullmans (presumably pushed to the side until required later in the day) and the welded rail attached with the familiar Pandrol railclip, which was a very new item of equipment at the time. (Photographer unknown)

Opposite: D1722 heads a collection of fine motive power at Swindon running shed in November 1964. Owing its size and latterly its existence largely to the presence of the Works, this shed had been closed to traffic that October and the red flags attached to the roof stanchions are obviously to remind drivers not to drive inside! We can assume that it had become a stabling point. The solitary steam engine No. 4903 'Astley Hall' had been withdrawn the previous month from Worcester shed and judging by the tail lamp has been towed from there, possibly en route to a scrapyard. The design of the Brush-built Type 4 was influenced by that of 'Lion', being the work of the Wilkes & Ashmore team who were also responsible for that of the 'Hymek', such as D7027 on the right. Further to the right of shot can be glimpsed an ex-GWR 'Dreadnought' twelve-wheel restaurant car previously used as office accommodation at the shed but now perhaps waiting to go to the Works for scrapping. (Nick Nicolson LN9-4-2)

Above: Alec Swain proceeded to a managerial role on the Western Region but one which still entitled him to ride on the footplate during various test runs of new rolling stock. Judging by the contents of his collection, he still made sure to have his camera with him on these occasions and a number of interesting scenes 'from the sharp end' are to be found in it. On 21 July 1966, D1923 has arrived at Westbury yard with a 7Z82 special working of new Freightliner wagons, apparently being overtaken by a Swindon Inter-City DMU bound for Bristol. The test crew are taking the opportunity to inspect the train and probably stretch their legs, after being confined to the cab for a while. Note the guards van coupled up at the rear; this was no high-speed test but may have been run in connection with the planned introduction of a Freightliner service between the London area and South Wales. (Alec Swain U77-4)

Opposite top: When the writer first saw this image, he thought he was looking at a locomotive in the early stages of being dismantled for scrap but the LMS prototype diesel No. 10000 is actually receiving major attention; this was at Brighton Works in the mid-1950s, during a spell on the Southern Region when its reliability had taken a turn for the worse. The fact that large sections of bodywork could be removed in this way shows how heavy the underframe was, being quite different in construction to later designs. It can also be noted that the Southern have classified this loco as '6P5F', instead of the 5P5F chosen by the LM. In the days before health and safety took a proper hold in workshops such as this, it was common to see items chalked with warning messages such as 'HOT'! (Photographer unknown)

Opposite bottom: Here we see the two prototype LMS-designed diesels enjoying their final fling on front line duties, just before the descendant English Electric Type 4 fleet began to take over on the WCML. Indeed, on the same day the photographer recorded D211 working through Cheddington on a stopping train to Bletchley – within a couple of years, roles would be reversed. The 'twins' are on the up fast with the southbound 'Royal Scot' in the bright sunshine of 20 June 1959. It is possible to stand on the same spot today while Pendolinos rush past and to see the concrete waiting shelter (behind the loco), still in use to this day. During electrification, the footbridge wasn't demolished but raised up on concrete pads in order to comply with the necessary clearances; it survived until 2013! The near platform now extends beyond where the signal box used to be to allow for a 12-car EMU to call here. (Donald Robertson DR37-1)

Type 5 Diesels and Prototypes

Above: After looking at the LMS prototypes, we must consider the Southern Railway's first foray into the world of diesel traction. No. 10203 was the last of its three locomotives to appear in traffic and by 16 July 1960, when this photo was taken, it was teamed up with the original two at Willesden depot. Apart from the Bulleid-Firth-Brown wheelsets, the bogies of this loco would feature again underneath the rather more handsome English Electric Type 4. That would also have the same 2000hp 16-cylinder engine, improved from the one originally rated at 1750hp in Nos. 10201 and 10202. Its class 7 power rating would put it on a par with a West Country Pacific or Royal Scot steam locomotive – no fireman needed, though! (Nick Nicolson LN3/60/5)

Opposite top: Some drivers were said to refer to No. 10800 as the 'wonder' locomotive, as in 'I wonder if it will work today'. Whether that was fair to it or not is unclear, but the pilot scheme versions which largely copied it, namely the D8400s, certainly never acquitted themselves well in service. Being produced by North British wasn't in its favour for a start, as history was to prove. No. 10800 is shown coming through Clapham Junction with the 10.18am from Brighton to Victoria on the kind of duty that was regarded as appropriate for a class 3 or 4 steam loco. Various points to note include the stovepipe chimney for the train heating boiler and that two worksplates seem to be attached above and below the number – the familiar diamond shape of the NBL one being above it. So much for the train – but why on earth should there be a garden roller on that platform? (Photographer unknown)

Opposite bottom: After several years out of use during the period when BR was receiving its first fleets of modern traction, in 1962 Brush purchased 10800 to use as a test bed for researching the performance of commutator-less traction motors. It was christened 'Hawk', although was never seen carrying that name. At the time, Brush had the foresight to believe that a.c. traction motors were the future, certainly for the higher powered (over 3000hp) locomotives envisaged to be needed then. The prediction was that a marginal increase in performance would be attained over a d.c. traction motor arrangement, for the same installed engine power, together with reduced maintenance costs and improved reliability. The loco's original Paxman 827hp engine was replaced with a Bristol Siddeley-Maybach 1400hp unit. A full description of the experiment was published in the June 1965 issue of '*Modern Railways*' and 'Hawk' is shown at Loughborough Works on 31 March 1965 (where a brand-new Type 4 is glimpsed behind). (Alec Swain R70-3)

Opposite top: Returning to a time when the alternative of gas turbine propulsion was still apparently being entertained by the Western Region, we find the Brown-Boveri produced No. 18000 at Paddington, on the point of being failed before departure with one of its regular workings, the 1.15pm to Weston super Mare. The date is 22 September 1959. The driver to the right (in overalls) is believed to be a Mr George Green of Old Oak Common; he seems to be in conversation with someone in the cab, as others wait for the inevitable decision. Meanwhile the fireman looks over the shoulder of a fitter investigating the trouble from the ballast. A Prairie tank engine would soon be hauling it off to the depot. On 15 April that year, 18000 had been noted working on only three of its four traction motors (its wheel arrangement being A1A-A1A), pending the arrival of a new armature from Switzerland. In the August, there was a report of the loco striking some lineside equipment, leading to it going to Swindon Works for repair and fitting of the armature. (Nick Nicolson LN2/10/2)

Opposite bottom: This close-up of part of the cabside of 18000 clearly shows its raised numerals and worksplate, together with the chromed handrails which tended to be slippery and were known to cause minor accidents. The date of this photo was 11 September 1960, by which time the Warship diesel-hydraulics were in service to the extent of thirty units or more and its presence on the WR was drawing to a close. Withdrawal from service followed at the end of that year. Gas turbine operation only made economic sense when locos were running at full power for most of the time and that wasn't possible in typical running conditions. (Alec Swain J46-6)

Above: Stepping a little further back in time, we find the other gas turbine tried out on the Western, namely No. 18100 from Metropolitan-Vickers. On 4 March 1952, it is topping Hemerdon Bank with a test train of twelve vehicles from Plymouth. The load was increased on successive days until it was found that 17 coaches could be comfortably taken over the South Devon banks. Both this loco and its Swiss competitor had been ordered by the Great Western Railway but delivered after nationalisation. The ample width of the 'six foot' is obvious in this view of a trackbed originally laid for Brunel's broad gauge. (A Lathey)

Above: 18100 made even less economic sense than 18000, running as it did on the more expensive fuel of kerosene, rather than heavy fuel oil. On 10 May 1953, the loco is off its wheels and in the middle of one of those not infrequent visits to Swindon Works for attention. Bogie fractures were one of the problems experienced, something which would cause headaches with several classes of modern traction. Having stood idle for a while after a failed attempt to convert it to burn heavy fuel oil, it was formerly taken out of service in 1957, some time before the first diesels appeared on the WR. After use as a test bed for a.c. electrical equipment and driver training on the first electrified sections of the WCML between Crewe and Manchester, it hung around in external storage at various locations before scrapping came in 1972. (Arthur Carpenter)

Opposite top: The prototype 'Deltic' was put on display at Battersea Wharf Goods Yard from 28 to 30 June 1957 as part of an exhibition to show how the BTC was progressing with its Modernisation Plan. At that time, this 3300hp monster was almost the only diesel locomotive that could be shown off under the plan – the other significant one was the English Electric Type 1. How remarkable then that nothing more powerful in the diesel sector would be seen until 'Kestrel' appeared in 1968 and that type would never go into production. On the design front, it is interesting to contrast the various styling cues evident in the loco and the cars parked nearby. There aren't too many straight lines but plenty of curved bodywork and all strongly influenced by American practice. In the shadow of a then active Battersea Power Station, the exhibition site was alongside Queenstown Road, somewhere that has long since been redeveloped. (Nick Nicolson LN1230)

Opposite bottom: Vanquisher meets vanquished at King's Cross on 10 May 1963, it would seem, as an un-named D9004 eases away from the terminus and passes an incoming A4 Pacific. Only a few weeks before, the section of the ECML south of Peterborough had been declared a steam-free zone. Unfortunately for BR, the combination of unreliability and insufficient delivery of new Brush Type 4 diesels had demanded a stay of execution; something which continued for much of the summer timetable. As for this Deltic, it received its 'Queen's Own Highlander' name a year later at Inverness. Note the speed limit stencils around the station throat; it has been suggested that fixing the ruling speed limit here to the single digit 8mph helped to save money on producing them! (Alec Swain N64-4)

'Traction Times'

Opposite top: On 17 August 1961, D9008 pulls off the main line at Darlington Bank Top and heads for the station platform. It is hauling the up 'Norseman', the train that ran between Tyne Commission Quay at Newcastle and King's Cross for the benefit of sea passengers from Norway. The locomotive had only entered traffic the previous month at Gateshead depot and would receive its 'The Green Howards' nameplates at Darlington two years later. Perhaps it isn't appreciated how long some Deltics ran in service in an un-named condition; the racehorse names were applied early, virtually always from new, whilst the last regimental name wasn't applied until September 1965. (Brian Wadey)

Opposite bottom: BRCW's Type 4 prototype 'Lion' (numbered D0260) sits inside Swindon Works alongside a Hymek diesel-hydraulic in an undated view (probably around 1963). The similarity in designs is obvious, which isn't surprising as both were drawn up by the Wilkes & Ashmore team at roughly the same time. Amidst some criticism that these didn't compare well to other designs, E G M 'Ted' Wilkes responded by saying that 'a locomotive does not have to be a streamlined projectile to be exciting to the enthusiast'. Nobody could accuse the manufacturer of making something boring though, as its all-over white livery ensured it was noticed wherever it went. Using the 2750hp Sulzer engine, 'Lion' was arguably the greatest influence on what BR eventually ordered for its standard Type 4. It was just unfortunate for BRCW that Brush was chosen as the supplier to produce this and they were never to build any more locomotives at their Smethwick Works, instead choosing to go into liquidation as a manufacturing business. (George Smith GS1/41/5)

Above: 'Lion' disappeared from the scene relatively quickly, once the D1500 series began to enter service. Somewhat strangely, another prototype named 'Falcon', with which it was competing, hung around in service for a few years afterwards and was even eventually taken into BR stock as the sole member of class 53. Originally numbered D0280 and released for tests in 1961, it shared some features with the Brush Type 2 but was rather spoilt by the prominence of its diagonal side-structure members, only partly redeemed by an interesting lime green and brown livery. It is shown at Bristol Bath Road on 15 February 1965, by which time it had been given a more standard two-tone green. Once a sufficiently powerful single unit had become available in the same power range, the twin-engined 2800hp 'Falcon' offered insufficient advantages over its competitors. Perhaps the fact that it used Maybach engines, similar to those in the Westerns, encouraged the Western Region to take it on for as long as it did. It saw use on Paddington to Bristol services at first and after renumbering as No. 1200 in 1970, ended its days working out of Newport's Ebbw Junction shed on local freight duties. Its presence at 'EJ' also ensured that many enthusiasts paid a visit there! (Alec Swain R35-6)

Above: The 2700hp English Electric DP2 advances northwards near Berkhamsted, heading the 'Emerald Isle Express' from London Euston to Llandudno and Holyhead on 11 May 1963. Using the same basic 16-cylinder engine as that in the 1948 LMS prototypes and 1958 Type 4 D200, though with charge air intercooling to considerably boost the power output, there was also commonality with the Type 3 D6700 and Deltics; the bodyshell was obviously similar to the latter's plus the bogie and traction motors were interchangeable with either. DP2 quickly gained a reputation for dependable service, clocking up higher mileages than just about any other diesel of the time. Sadly, this evidence came a little too late to change the minds of BR whose traction engineers opted to order Brush Type 4s in quantity off the drawing board. It was also known that the Chief Mechanical & Electrical Engineer Mr J F Harrison had a preference for a flat fronted design of locomotive. EE had reduced their design's production costs by using a Deltic bodyshell but to no avail. However, some years later of course, they were successful in winning an order for fifty Type 4s based heavily on the DP2's mechanicals, albeit to be supplied on hire. All the ingredients for success were there – what a pity that '*Modern Railways*' had reason to state that 'the gadgetry which BR has applied to the production DP2s has turned an essentially simple, economical design into an expensive box of tricks which is probably unsaleable outside Britain'. (Jim Harbart FH1885)

Shunters

Above: Photographer George Bett was living in Dundee at the time this North British Locomotive Co. shunter was introduced to work in Dundee's docks in August 1955. On 4 October that year, we find two crew members still clearly enjoying using their new steed. Labelled as class D2/1 by BR in the pre-TOPS age, Nos. 11700-11702 had been built in 1953-54, followed by 11703-11707 using the same 200hp Paxman engine and Voith hydraulic transmission. The later batch had a larger cab and oval buffers instead of circular ones, though all proved unsuccessful in service and were withdrawn by 1968, carrying Nos. D2700 -2707. The production series of 73 units (with a 225hp engine and lowered bonnet) were no more fortunate, being taken out of service en masse in the same period, as much through lack of work and a policy of standardisation than through poor performance. A similar loco from private industry service and numbered D2700 (not the original loco which was scrapped) exists in preservation at the Colne Valley Railway. (George Bett GCB521C)

Opposite bottom: 'Kestrel', No. HS4000, making its first demonstration run from Marylebone to Princes Risborough and back on 27 January 1968. Announced as the world's most powerful single-engined diesel locomotive, it was well-designed and clearly very capable, having the advantage of reduced maintenance costs when compared to a twin-engined Deltic. The aim was to provide BR with a mixed traffic diesel that could accommodate future increases in line speeds, as well as expected drains on engine power like the demands of air-conditioning. An additional improved feature was the driver's cab with its resilient mountings, better sound insulation and air pressurisation. However, it was to be let down by a very high axle loading and the substituting of Class 47 style bogies for the heavy Commonwealth type failed to address this. BR lost interest, choosing to pursue a multiple-unit style of train for future high-speed passenger services. (Alec Swain W83-6)

Opposite top: Brand new BR 0-6-0 shunter D2030 sparkles in the sunshine outside Swindon Works on 28 October 1958. This became the standard small shunter, although it was basically the same as the tried and tested Drewry model (which later became class 04) with just a few detail differences. It sports the original style of conical 'Noddy' exhaust stack, only fitted to the first 33 of the class. The story was that Swindon wished to fit copper capped chimneys to them at first! Note the full stop after the 'D' prefix, seemingly not applied to other shunters or locos which had their numbers applied in the traditional Gill Sans style. Also worth pointing out is the fact that the drive from the gearbox hasn't been connected; perhaps this was because it was to be towed to its first depot, Cambridge. Despite being of the preferred type, D2030 never received a TOPS number, being withdrawn from Brighton in 1969 and scrapped soon after. (Nick Nicolson LN2047)

Opposite bottom: Let's look back to a time when railways were allowed into our towns to serve industry on a smaller scale, with on-street running and weed-strewn formations that snaked in amongst terraced housing to reach coal yards and dockside warehousing. A selection of small shunters now follows, sometimes mixing it with the local traffic and doubtless attracting a few curses from the more impatient motorists; all so unlike today where rail tracks must seemingly be held in their own mini-fortress of steel and mesh. D2210 starts us off by holding up a Ford Prefect and a Zodiac (plus a bike and a Morris Commercial) on a trip to Great Yarmouth Docks with a rake of bogie bolster wagons. The location is Hall Quay and the wagons are being tripped alongside the River Yare to the South Quay. We are lucky that Dr Ian Allen bothered to record such scenes for us at a time when there was still plenty of steam out on the main lines, even if he didn't seem to carry a notebook with him. Unfortunately, this means that many views are undated; however, the writer believes this one may be from 1961, shortly before the loco was transferred from Yarmouth to Lowestoft. We are grateful to former East Anglian railwayman Andy Wallis for his assistance in filling in some of the detail. (Dr Ian Allen ICA D460)

Above: Staying in Yarmouth, we find D2032 calling at the coal concentration depot at Swan Yard. This was reached via the streets and through a narrow gap between a house and the White Swan Inn, known to railwaymen as the 'Hole in the Wall'. Originally part of the Yarmouth Union Railway (connecting the town's main stations), the through route was truncated beyond the gates in the background. This picture is full of content. Apart from the bags of coal stacked rather precariously to one side and the typical sort of detritus lying amongst the rails, operations have attracted some attention from the house behind – a youngster looks from one window while Mum watches from another. One suspects that this is nothing unusual to them but the presence of a gentleman in a suit, holding a camera, certainly is. Drewry class 04 shunters were common in the Yarmouth area after steam but as withdrawals decimated their number, the standard BR built class 03s predominated and saw out these operations to closure in the 1970s. (Dr Ian Allen ICA D594)

Above: With limited space at the other end of the coal yard, some shunting manoeuvres involved going back through the gap and across the road again; the limited width of the 'Hole in the Wall' can now be appreciated! Because several motor vehicle registration plates are on display in this view, we can date it to around 1968/69. Today, the road layout has been greatly simplified. The whole terrace of houses on the right has gone and the A149 North Quay road now sweeps past the pub where the 'Hole' and coal yard used to be. Only the pub itself (no longer affiliated to the Steward & Patteson brewery) and the North Tower remain from this view. As for D2032, shedded at Norwich for its entire service with BR, it was withdrawn in 1971 before going on to spend a much longer working life in Italy. (Dr Ian Allen ICA D271)

Opposite top: An unidentified early series class 03 picks its way behind the houses of Kimberley Road as it returns along the Lowestoft South Side branch with empty wagons. The radiator appears to have a half-cover over it, possibly to enhance colder weather performance. Another stand-out feature is obviously the double-sided and fixed semaphore signal, which only appears to be lit on the one side. Durban Road crossing was towards the rear of the train (a flagman can just be picked out there), so it may only need to have been lit for trains approaching from this side. The date is indeterminate but likely to have been in the mid to late 1960s; this stretch of track finally closing in 1972 when Boulton & Paul ceased using rail transport. (Dr Ian Allen ICA D1118)

Opposite bottom: In his pictorial book *'Diesels in East Anglia'* Dr Allen spoke of taking railway photographs 'on his rounds', no doubt receiving tip offs about unusual workings, and it is quite apparent that local footplate crews recognised him wherever he went. The stretch of tramway seen here ran along Riverside Road in Lowestoft and was a spur off the South Side branch, serving the Boulton & Paul factory, towards which D2563 appears to be pushing brake van B952594. It would return with wagons loaded with timber products. All the food processing buildings beyond were ultimately demolished to leave something of a waste ground here, with no trace of the track at this point. Studying the area on Google Earth, however, reveals that two sidings inside the abandoned factory site are still extant. Readers are recommended to study further examples of Dr Allen's work in *'First Generation Diesels in East Anglia'* by Alan C Butcher, also published by Transport Treasury publishing. (Dr Ian Allen ICA D1041)

Above: We now come to the famed Wisbech and Upwell Tramway. Although it did carry passengers at first, its principal task was to serve the agricultural producers of that area of the Fens. Becoming dieselised in 1952, long before the Modernisation Plan, the tramway was nevertheless a visual treat for the railway photographer. Drewry built shunter D2201 represented one of the first 0-6-0 diesel-mechanical designs that would soon see service across the country in their hundreds. It employed the same 204hp Gardner engine used in similar types of shunter from various manufacturers. It is seen passing through the village of Outwell, heading for the yard at Upwell with a brake van. As for the Austin Cambridge owned by Dr Allen, this was arguably a choice of the more mature motorist (the writer's grandfather owned a white one, with a maroon stripe!); it was a comfortable car featuring leather seats and lots of chrome, but only a modest performance. The British Motor Corporation produced them for nearly a whole decade. 364 URT is parked outside a shop belonging to Norman R Nelson selling 'quality fish and chips' (and in business to this day). In those days, shop frontages tended to be rather plain; sometimes just taking down the sign and giving it a lick of paint would leave a building looking like any other house in the street. (Dr Ian Allen D965)

Opposite bottom: It's clear that people living in houses along this road could literally step out of their front doors, only to be confronted by a freight train! D2202 is captured with just a couple of vans in tow, probably not long before the tramway's closure in May 1966. Don't get the impression that this had always been a typical load; in the 1950s, trains of up to 40 wagons would be a common sight being wheeled across the landscape. The yard at Upwell was extensive with eleven sidings at one time; inward traffic tended to be coal, whilst outward was a wide range of food produce, including strawberries in season. Nos. 11101 to 11103 (eventually class 04 D2201 to D2203) were allocated to March depot and equipped to work the tramway. Board of Trade regulations demanded that locomotives were fitted with sideplates and cowcatchers. After the first fifteen of this class had been constructed, later built shunters of this variety had greater diameter wheels fitted, together with larger windows and circular buffers, all making for quite a different looking product. (Dr Ian Allen D1075)

Above: Messrs Hunslet supplied 120 shunters that also employed the trusty Gardner eight-cylinder power unit. Their name was emblazoned on a plate whose width extended right across the top of the radiator, presumably to avoid confusion with the rest! What would eventually become a class 05 (though only one of them stayed in BR service long enough to carry the '05'), No. 11141 is seen waiting near to Lowestoft Coke Ovens signal box. During the 1960s, BR divested itself of a huge amount of freight business, especially that in the general merchandise sector. The Beeching Report didn't only bring about the closure of branch lines, it also rejected many of the smaller or occasional traffics for which shunters were often the most appropriate motive power. The fact that rail transport was known (even then) to be more environmentally friendly didn't matter to anyone. Britain's commercial vehicle sector was booming in those days. The writer recalls noting the variety of manufacturers' names of trucks on a motorway journey at the time: ERF, Scammell, Foden, Seddon Atkinson, Leyland, Dodge, Guy, Bedford, Karrier, Albion, Commer. With that amount of competition, BR was always going to be struggling to retain its market share. (Dr Ian Allen D1395)

Above: In similar fashion to the Drewry class 04, the last batch of Hunslet 0-6-0s were decidedly different from the earlier builds. Larger diameter wheels and revised gearing changed the tractive effort and also allowed for higher top speed. D2617 is pictured at Knottingley with a trip working on 20 September 1965. Also apparent is the larger area of window glass, probably serving to make the cab like a greenhouse in the summer. At its peak in 1966, BR's total fleet of shunting locomotives came to over 1800. The National Traction Plan of 1967 cut this number by half over the following four years or so. Whilst many were wastefully scrapped, industrial users were presented with a bonanza of useful motive power, resulting in the demand for new locos being severely depressed. (Alec Swain T40-3)

Opposite top: The fourteen diesel-hydraulic 0-4-0 shunters supplied by NBL in 1958 were doomed to an even quicker exit from the scene than their main line relatives on the Western Region; all had been withdrawn and scrapped by the close of 1967. Fitted with a comparatively powerful 330hp MAN engine, all were allocated to Devons Road in East London, well-known for being BR's first motive power depot to be completely dieselised in the same year. This is where we find D2901 and D2902 in an undated shot, likely to have been taken at the weekend when their presence around the docks wasn't required. In October 1962, *'Modern Railways'* magazine stated that early problems with the hydraulic transmission had been resolved but the shunter's excessive overhang led to broken springs and much vertical oscillation. The depot's spell in the limelight was to prove a short one as in 1964 BR decided that other installations could cover its declining workload. The shed was eventually demolished in the 1970s and the land redeveloped. (George Smith GS1/79/5)

Opposite bottom: Four days after being handed over to the Science Museum, the famous first member of C B Collett's 'Castle' class of locomotives, 4073 'Caerphilly Castle', leaves the railway network at Park Royal on 3 June 1961, with the willing assistance of a relatively new D4004 of the BR/EE 350hp series of diesel-electric 0-6-0 shunters. In his book *'British Rail, Fleet Survey No.7'*, Brian Haresnape wrote that 'no words of praise could rate too highly these tough and reliable machines' and it is hard to disagree. They were essentially based on the LMS design of 1944, though of course all the four pre-nationalisation companies had tried their own similar versions and lessons were learned from them too. Whilst the English Electric engine had proved itself already, BR chose to try Lister/ Blackstone and Crossley power units of the same rating as well; all were to be victims of the late 1960s shunter cull. Construction took place from 1952 to 1962 at no less than five different BR Workshops: Crewe, Horwich, Doncaster, Darlington and Derby. Under TOPS, the vast majority were classed 08 and a handful (with higher gearing to give an improved top speed) given class 09. Six were grouped into three pairs to work as 'master and slave' units at Tinsley hump yard, the class 13s. The 146 Blackstone-engined ones were allocated class 10; all had been withdrawn by the end of 1972 and so never carried their new numbers. However, with several going into industrial service, four have ended up in preservation. Classes 11 and 12 were reserved for the similar designs built for the LMS and SR respectively, also destined never to carry their new numbers. (R C Riley RCR15828)

Shunters

Above: This photo illustrates the advantage of the 0-4-0 brand of diesel shunter. The tight curves evident amongst the dockside cranes at Aberdeen were no place for BR's standard types, meaning that the Barclay class 06 (as these shunters became) enjoyed something of an extended life in Scotland, whilst most of the other minority types had fallen by the wayside. The shortest-lived loco of its class was No. D2441. New in 1960, it had been scrapped by the end of 1967. D2420 (shown here) however, managed to survive to be renumbered 06003 and once again (as a departmental loco) to 97804, being withdrawn in 1984; it is now preserved by the Heritage Shunters Trust at Peak Rail, Rowsley. The date of the photo is 4 November 1967, when the Great North of Scotland Railway Association arranged their police-escorted brake van tour. There is colour footage of the occasion to be enjoyed on YouTube. (Norris Forrest NF275-08)

Opposite top: We'll take one more look at a member of this long-lived class of shunter. D4192 was the very last of the line, completed at Darlington in August 1962. Here we find it on an unusual task, hauling the RCTS 'Silvertown Tramway' railtour of 30 March 1963 close to St Mark's Church, Silvertown (now known as the Brick Lane Music Hall). Although the general consensus of opinion was that these locos were practically unbreakable, shunter drivers needed to know what they could reasonably expect from them, if they weren't to incur damage to the traction equipment. The flexibility of the design however, meant that they were as well-suited to moving single parcels vans around stations as to heaving long freight consists over the humps of marshalling yards. They were often called up to haul passenger trains on branch lines and that's what many preserved examples still do on private railways today. It is perhaps only current heightened concerns about the environment which has seen their removal from widespread network usage; therefore, the sight of one quietly ticking over in a siding somewhere is now a rarity. (Alec Swain N16/1)

Opposite bottom: Railway engineering departments often possessed their own shunters, possibly to ensure they weren't borrowed for use elsewhere, as could happen with regular fleet locomotives. Shown is ED2 at Derby in 1961, one of a type ordered from John Fowler & Co. at an early stage under the auspices of the LMS, but mostly appearing after nationalisation. An 0-4-0 diesel-mechanical of only 150hp, it saw use by the civil engineers and was originally thought to have been scrapped at Derby Works in 1965. Evidence subsequently came to light that it survived for another three years before meeting its end at a Rotherham scrapyard. Many of a similar arrangement were ordered by the military during the war. There is no obvious exhaust to be seen but the radiator filler cap certainly stands out! (Canon Alec George AG68-4)

EMUs

Above: On 22 July 1968, M28571M leads a service from Manchester Oxford Road into Altrincham. M29650M was the centre car (with first class compartments) and M29232M brought up the rear. It is believed that in their earlier days, there were even some ladies-only compartments. This would suggest that the operator was very concerned about providing the right commuting experience for all its customers, considering how short the journey was in terms of time and distance! These class 505 units lasted until April 1971, after forty years' service, and this particular set ran in all-over blue livery with full yellow ends for its final two years. Introduced by the Manchester, South Junction and Altrincham Railway on a route wired at 1500V DC, the sets initially came under the joint auspices of the LMS and LNER. Withdrawal came after 25kV AC operation was extended to Altrincham, allowing the use of class 304 (AM4)

EMUs. Note the unusually clean buffers on this unit and the lower quadrant starting signal on the platform. Photographer Alec Swain used this image in part 11 of the *'BR Fleet Survey'* of books; he had compiled the latter part of the overall work in 1989 for publisher Ian Allan, following the death of Brian Haresnape. (Alec Swain Y21-5)

Opposite bottom: New AM5 four-car EMU No. 516 runs onto the single line section through Ware station on the Hertford East branch on 5 November 1960. Introduction of the full electric service over this line was due to commence later that month. Although these units had received attention from BR's Design Panel, their all-over dark green livery led to a rather drab appearance from the start. Gresley bogies were a feature of this (TOPS class 305) and similarly designed AC and DC units. On completion of the West Anglia Route Modernisation scheme (centralising control at

Liverpool Street), the signal box at Ware was boarded up and then demolished in 2009. It had been completed only a few months before this photograph was taken and, with its characteristic sun shades, had been considered for listing as a building of historic interest. (Leslie Freeman LRF5280)

This page, top: With the introduction of Glasgow's 'Blue Trains' on many Clydeside services, there could hardly have been a greater change in the travel experience being offered there by BR. Passengers went from using steam-hauled non-corridor stock to the latest electric multiple units, with open saloons where it was even possible to look over the driver's shoulder. Things weren't all plain sailing, of course, due to the well-known withdrawal in late 1960 of the entire fleet following serious problems with their transformers. Sadly the pleasure of a forward-facing view wasn't to last either, once the novelty wore off and drivers decided they preferred their privacy behind the roller blind. This view from March 1960 shows a new unit (headed by Sc75582) at Jordanhill, as the flat-capped driver and guard are changing ends during a shakedown run. The AM3 (eventually class 303) units sported sliding doors, in contrast to most other new designs which persisted with traditional slam doors, yet the bogie design was still based on the Gresley-type. This particular unit is so new that the destination and route indicator blinds haven't been fitted yet. (WAC Smith W54178)

This page bottom: Moving down south to Basingstoke, we find another new EMU being put through trials before its entry into service. Or do we? This unit carried no power equipment, after all! On 20 August 1966, S76280 heads 4TC unit No. 406 with class 33 No. D6516 hauling it, judging by the tail-lamp at this end. The 'TC' stood for 'Trailer Composite'. These coaches were conversions from ordinary hauled Mk1 stock and equipped with the latest B5 bogie. As part of the Bournemouth electrification scheme, their normal employment was to be coupled to a powered 4-REP set from Waterloo and then passed over to a class 33 for the unelectrified leg on to Weymouth; their advantage being that they could be driven regardless of what was providing the traction. Curiously, polished aluminium BR logos were fitted to the cabs, instead of the usual white transfers, the livery being a matt blue livery with small yellow warning panel in the gangway door bay. Three shorter 3-TC sets were also created, though these were later enhanced with an extra coach to bring them into line with the rest so giving 31 sets in total. D6516 was one of the earlier locomotives to be converted for push-pull operation, having been a Hither Green engine before its transfer to Eastleigh in April of 1966; it would later become 33104 under TOPS renumbering. Basingstoke's new power signal box (the white building) may be seen beyond the semaphore gantry behind the bridge in the background, the manual signalling then still being controlled by the old Basingstoke 'A' box out of sight to the left. The down and the up fast lines appear to have been relaid with concrete sleepers and continuously welded rail, so passengers would soon be enjoying an all-round quieter and smoother ride to what they'd been accustomed to. (Alec Swain U85-4)

Electric Locos

Above: Third rail electric locomotive No. 20003 is pictured parked in a siding at Barnham on 17 June 1961. The kindest thing to say about the three d.c. Co-Co electrics in this series (produced between 1941 and 1948) would be that they were functional; if there was a prize awarded for the ugliest example of modern traction, they would have to be contenders. Even so they gave useful service to the Southern Region, expected to be labelled class 70 under TOPS, but were always likely to fall victim to economies, and being such a small class; withdrawal came during 1969. The chime whistle on the loco's roof would later be replaced by twin air horns and a small headcode panel inserted between the front windows. The mid-roof pantograph could be used in a handful of goods yards where an overhead wire was provided for safer operations. Immediately to the left of this view became the site of a nasty accident the following year on 1 August, when 2-BIL unit No. 2088 was derailed working a Brighton to Portsmouth Harbour train: A point motor fault caused by a freak electrical mis-connection led to a facing point being partially open as this approached, serving to flip the front coach over (as it approached the station platform) and derailing the second. Luckily, the train was in the process of regaining speed after a signal check and an alert driver had spotted the points in time to begin a brake application. There were no serious injuries. (A E Bennett AEB5666)

Opposite top: A side-on view of 26016 at Wath on 19 September 1954 shows how large the bogies were on the EM1. These took up practically the whole of the space underneath the bodywork and were coupled together, independently of the bodywork. Early issues with weight transfer during acceleration were ironed out by electrical modifications, making the locos more sure-footed. A twin pantograph arrangement was chosen initially with the idea of using separate ones for either direction of travel; in the event, both were used at the same time to help overcome any problems with dirty contact wires. Wath yard was the principal stabling point for these locos on the eastern side of the Pennines and Sunday visits to this installation would be guaranteed to witness at least half a dozen of them, almost up to the closure of the Woodhead route in 1981. (Arthur Carpenter).

Right: Chairman of the British Transport Commission, Sir Brian Robertson, chats to the driver of EM2 No. 27000 at Sheffield Victoria upon the inauguration of electrified services to Manchester (London Road) on 14 September 1954. General Robertson served in both World Wars and was offered the job at the BTC in 1953, a post which he held until 1961, when Dr Beeching took over. To this day, many ex-service personnel go on to second careers on our railways, though not often to such high managerial positions! This image is one of the glass plates in the Transport Treasury collection - perhaps surprisingly, this form of photography was still in use by the press right into the 1960s. Another plate illustrates a huge gathering of railway VIPs and dignitaries at the opening of the Woodhead Tunnel on 3 June 1954. (Photographer unknown).

Opposite: On 14 March 1958, EM2 Co-Co electric locomotive 27006 pulls out of Manchester London Road station with what is almost certainly a service to Sheffield, as they performed few other duties. At first sight, the EM2 appears to be an enlargement of the EM1 but there are significant differences in the running gear. The buffers and coupling are attached to the body, rather than the bogie, whilst the bogie itself is of a more advanced post-war design and similar to that employed on the LMS diesels 10000 & 10001. In common with the Bo-Bo EM1 though, they were certainly well equipped with sand boxes. Rated at 2490hp and capable of 90mph, the EM2s were rarely stretched on Woodhead route services. They had been devised in anticipation of further main line DC electrification on the national network. However, rapid advances in the development of high voltage AC systems (proven in other countries, such as France) led to a decision to standardise on 25kV AC for all future major electrification schemes. As is well known, the EM2s were briefly re-classified under TOPS as class 77 just as they were retired from BR in 1968 and sold on to the Dutch Railways. (Jim Flint 1541).

Above: This shot of the nameplate area of 26054 'Pluto' in August 1968 shows the heavily rivetted construction of this Gresley-designed locomotive, together with the later design of British Railways crest with lion and crown mounted on a separate plate. Patronage on the passenger service between Manchester and Sheffield never lived up to expectations and was under threat of closure several times. Generally speaking, at that time people didn't commute long distances to work. Anyone working in Sheffield tended to live in the Sheffield area too, whereas today there is far more trans-Pennine commuting. After the withdrawal of the under-utilised EM2s, it was the boiler-fitted contingent of the EM1s which were largely responsible for powering these services up to their cessation in 1970.
(Alec Swain Y35-4)

Above: The AL4 a.c. electric locomotive represented GEC's contribution to the competition to establish a standard locomotive design for the West Coast Main Line electrification that was being progressed in the early 1960s, construction being subcontracted to North British in Glasgow. Here we have No. E3037 on display at Marylebone Goods Yard on 27 April 1960 for the press and rail industry delegates (with E5012 and D5081 parked behind). John Beresford-Evans of the Design Research Unit had produced an outline for how this would look and five manufacturers each came up with their own finished product. At first glance, AL1 to AL5 all looked pretty much the same but there were detail differences, especially in the arrangement of grills on the bodyside and equipment within. Uniquely, the marginally more attractive AL4 exhibited four small droplight windows on one side and oval buffers. A feature apparent on some of the first produced a.c. electrics was the non-standard configuration of digits on their four-character headcode panels, a letter being shown in the first position rather than the second, as would become the norm. (Nick Nicolson LN2/100/4)

Opposite top: Consecutively numbered members of the AL1 class (built by BRCW in Birmingham), Nos. E3015 and E3016, pull away from Crewe in July 1961, heading for Manchester Piccadilly at a time when this was the first section of line permitting full working by 25kV a.c. electric traction on the LMR. Note the ex-LMS coach heading the formation. It's fair to say that the enhanced performance delivered by electric traction at the time was a revelation. The smooth and rapid acceleration, together with relative quietness of operation, was a complete contrast to that of both steam and diesel power. The expense of the LMR electrification scheme however was to cause disquiet at the Transport Ministry and for a time it was paused for a review; when BR Chairman Dr Beeching paid a visit to Crewe to inspect what had been done, he commented that 'they have put washing lines above every track!' In later years, electrification of a route would come to be used as an opportunity to simplify track layouts and reduce costs. One little known fact is that much of the copper from scrapped steam loco fireboxes ended up being used in contact wire production. (Alec Swain K77-4)

Opposite bottom: E3071 has been brought to Derby on 25 July 1962 for fitting out with cabling prior to a test. It is unknown what the precise nature of the testing was in this case, though the location is believed to be close to the Way and Works signal box on the site where BR's Railway Technical Centre would ultimately be established in 1964. The Alsthom-type bogie seen here was also employed underneath the AL1, though the AL5 series of locos came from BR's Doncaster Works. The other two types of locos, the AL2 and AL3, were built by Beyer Peacock (Gorton) and English Electric (Vulcan Foundry) respectively. A number of problems were to be experienced with the mercury arc rectifiers on the AL3 and AL4 locos and after 1967 they were put into store, as it was found that enough units were available to meet requirements, once the later AL6 had entered squadron service. (Alec Swain M30-3)

Opposite top: Inside Crewe Works, AL1 No. E3022 has probably just received its first full overhaul and is now being prepared for its return to service on 12 February 1967. The vacuum brake system is being tested at this point. Although BR's corporate blue livery was being applied to diesels by this time, the loco seems to have retained its original 'electric blue' livery, although it has lost one of its two pantographs as operating experience had proved that there was little advantage in having two. The obligatory overhead warning flashes have yet to be applied. (Eric Sawford ES6027)

Opposite bottom: From March to November 1964, Nuneaton was a motive power switchover point for many expresses on the 'Western Lines' of the London Midland Region. This had followed a 61 route-mile extension of the wires, southwards from Crewe. A handful of long-distance services remained diesel hauled throughout but several Scottish-bound services such as this one (the 1.30pm from Euston on 18 August), being taken over by AL5 No. E3089, underwent two changes; one here and another at Crewe. It would almost certainly have relieved an EE Type 4 and may well have handed its train over to a Britannia Pacific when it reached Crewe. In those days, changing of locos during a train's journey was routine whereas today it is unusual (not least because of fixed formations) and generally avoided to save time and expense. (Alec Swain Q52-5)

Above: The one hundred AL6 Bo-Bo electrics (to be class 86) were regarded as BR's standard a.c. electric loco for use on all future overhead electrified routes. Construction was shared between Doncaster Works and the Vulcan Foundry of English Electric. Quite heavily influenced by the AL5 model, these differed outwardly by being slightly longer and having a stepped front end. They also incorporated axle-hung traction motors, which led to very poor riding qualities and a fair amount of grief for the track engineers too. Much work was to follow on this design's suspension! On 8 March 1965, the first production example from EE's works No. E3161 (featuring a cross arm pantograph) passes Stafford on a trial run. The driver appears to be alone in the cab, though one suspects that other staff are likely to be elsewhere on the loco. On the same day, E3101 of the Doncaster-built batch was seen at Crewe. The later class 87 that was built in anticipation of the wires extending from Crewe to Glasgow was effectively an improved AL6. (Alec Swain R61-3)

Bibliography

The following books/ magazines and websites have been consulted:

Book of the Warships, J. Jennison: Irwell Press 2009
BR Fleet Survey series, B. Haresnape & A. Swain: Ian Allan, 1981-1990
British Rail Designed 1948-97, D. Lawrence: Ian Allan 2016
Diesels in East Anglia, Dr I.A. Allen: OPC 1980
Diesels – a Driver's Reminiscences, L.C. Jacks: Bradford Barton 1982
Diesel Pioneers, David N Clough: Ian Allan 2005
First Generation Diesels in East Anglia, Alan Butcher: Transport Treasury Publishing 2020
Locomotive Testing on Britain's Railways 1901-1968, D. Peel: Kestrel Railway Books 2013
Rail-online.co.uk
Railways in the Blood, R.H.N. Hardy: Ian Allan 1985
The Allocation History of BR Diesels and Electrics, R. Harris: Self published 1983
The Railway Magazine - various issues.
The Southern Way Special Issue 16 (50 Years of the Bournemouth Electrics), Colin Scott-Morton:
Crecy Publishing 2019
The Western's Hydraulics, J.K. Lewis: Book Law 2006
Trains Illustrated / Modern Railways - various issues.
Six Bells Junction website.

Certain signal boxes around the land offered not only a good view of the railway but also one of the surrounding area. Factory Junction in South London would appear to be a case in point, though any duty signalman here would probably have little time to take it in, except perhaps on a quiet Sunday morning shift. There is detail aplenty to be seen, ranging from the yard staff pausing from their labours as they watch the passing train to the familiar outline of Battersea Power Station smoking away in the distance. A very new 'Hastings' DEMU set No. 1003 is caught by the camera on 27 February 1957. It is thought this was en route from Eastleigh Works to Bexhill in order to undertake some publicity photography, as these sets were due for introduction into service that spring. Brian Haresnape, ever with his eye on design, pointed out the train's plain livery and 'very basic front end design ... typical of Eastleigh's lack of attention to aesthetic details'. Harsh criticism or fair, these units went on to give long service on BR's Southern Region and we have a preserved set still running on the main line today, of course. (Dick Riley RCR10240)